CHILD LOSS
The Heartbreak and the Hope

CLARA HINTON

For all the amazing people I've met, and those I haven't, who struggle every day to find hope.

A special thanks from deep within to my eleven heroes who are my strength when life lets me down.

Shugs, I love you. More. And, even more.

ACKNOWLEDGMENTS

To my daughter Alex whose heart is bigger than the ocean and shares in her mom's dreams. You never told me it couldn't be done. Instead, you walked alongside of me, pushing me forward a thousand times when I said I was too weary to keep going.

Without you, this book would not be.

And, I will be forever grateful. I love you.

CONTENTS

INTRODUCTION

My first experience with child loss happened when I was fifteen years old. On a warm summer evening in June of 1965 my thirteen-year-old sister Carmella died. I can remember every moment of how the news of her death was delivered to my mother from the two state policemen standing on our porch waiting for us to pull into our driveway.

I was sitting in the front seat of our car next to my mother, and she turned her face towards me before getting out of the car and said, "Your sister is dead." And, that was the moment that will be forever engraved upon my heart.

My sister had been living in a place called the Betty Bacharach Home by the Sea for the last six months of her life. I was told she went there to get better from her asthma, but the truth is she went there to die. My parents felt I was too young to hear the truth, and by keeping the truth from me the trauma of her death was magnified a thousand times over.

Years passed, and time allowed the pain of my sister's death to grow less raw, but there was always an inner fear that haunted me. I was acutely aware of death and the painful void that was created when a loved one leaves us. My daily prayer was that I would never have to experience this kind of pain in my life when I had a family of my own.

We know that prayers are not always answered according to our purposes, and life does not always turn out as we dream and plan.

After I married and experienced the pure miracle of the birth of my first child, a daughter, I breathed a sigh of relief. Life was good! Life was beautiful, amazing, and so full of rich and wonderful blessings.

How naïve we become in our thinking!

My life has been blessed with a beautiful family, but not without great sorrow and pain. Following several miscarriages, I delivered a stillborn baby boy, Samuel. He was perfect beyond words and precious in every way. When I held this child in my arms saying both my hello and my good-bye on the very same day, my heart broke so much that I truly believed it was beyond repair. It took years for me to regain even a small amount of trust in life again. My innocence had truly been stolen away.

Following the heartbreak of a broken marriage, my living children continued to fill my life with beauty, passion and purpose, and once again I believed that life was good!

The fears I had when the children were small seemed to vanish when they reached adulthood, and no longer did I feel that ominous cloud of darkness lingering overhead.

That all changed on the evening of May 22, 2015.

On a warm spring evening, following a visit to the cemetery with some friends who were visiting their son's grave site, I was home reading in bed and saying a prayer of deep, meaningful, sincere thanks for the blessing and safety of my children when the phone rang.

I looked to see who was calling, and instinctively my body became rigid, and I found it almost impossible to answer the phone. Deep in my heart, I knew this was not a call that I wanted to take.

"They tried. They tried for over an hour. But, they couldn't save him."

I fell to the floor screaming out in agony to God. Once again, a child of mine had been taken away. My firstborn son died unexpectedly of a massive heart attack at the early age of forty-two leaving behind a wife and three young children that were the love of his life.

The words in this book are words written from the very depths of my heart. For over twenty-five years I have devoted a large portion of my life working with bereaved parents and families who have lost a child. Because resources were so few in my early days of grief and loss, I made a promise that I would work hard to educate others about this journey we call grief. I vowed that I would make sure others had available tools that could help them travel this road of grief better equipped to help them not only survive but to learn how to re-enter life again.

I have traveled this path of child loss several times over now, and I can say to you with all sincerity and truth that there is hope beyond the heartbreak!

With love,

Clara Hinton

1 ENTERING THE FOGGY ABYSS OF GRIEF

Receiving word that your child has died is traumatic. There is nothing that can ever fully prepare you for that moment when you hear your child's life on this earth has ended.

I can think of no other loss comparable to child loss. The pain a parent suffers is immeasurable. There is nothing that can ever fully prepare you for that moment when you hear your child's life on this earth has ended. We immediately go into a temporary denial after hearing of the death of our child, and our world as we once knew it is shattered, torn apart, and leaves us in a dark place spinning upside down and totally out of control with our emotions and thoughts. Our breath is literally taken away and we momentarily forget how to breathe.

And, the truth is that for a while we don't want to breathe.

Even when there are warnings that our child could die such as in the case of a lingering illness, drug addiction, or severe mental depression, we live in a state of denial because the possibility of our child dying is too much for our human minds to process. The love we have for our child prevents us from entering "that place" in our thoughts.

1

When we hear of other parents losing a child, our intelligence tells us that child loss happens. And, we feel sad. We understand to a very small degree that this is a pain that we never want to have come into our own lives. So, we avoid the topic of child loss if at all possible. The only time we really get involved in a small way is when the child of a friend or family member dies. Then, the reality of child loss becomes real, but it is still in a very distant kind of way.

We know that children die every day. We read about children dying in our local newspapers. We hear about children dying on social medial. We hear about children dying due to illness, accidents, overdoses, and premature births, complications of surgery, drownings, murders, and natural causes.

But, still our minds protect us and say, "Not my child." We will not allow our minds to ever think of the possibility that our child could die before we, the parents, do. That thought is much too painful to entertain.

So we keep our minds busy. We pause when we hear of the death of a child long enough to feel momentarily sad. We might even dwell on the child's death for a while longer if we know the child. But, human nature is to go back about our business saying something like, "Thank God that didn't happen to me. I don't know what I'd do if I ever lost my child."

We close our eyes at night, and all is well once again. Our minds protect us from harmful thoughts because that's the way we were designed.

What happens when we are the ones who receive the news? What happens when tragedy strikes and it is our child that dies? How do we process this? How do we handle this news?

Our reactions to the news of our child's death are different for everyone and can range from the total silence of shock, passing out, all the way to releasing blood-curdling screams. *One thing is certain, though. We are all led to the same place – the foggy abyss of grief.*

What exactly is this foggy abyss? Having entered this abyss far too many times, I can only describe it as a temporary holding place. It's that place we enter for protection for a while as we process exactly what has happened. The abyss is a place of temporary refuge from a tragedy that has caused heartbreak. The abyss is an emotional hiding place where we can rest our pain for a while. The abyss is a place where we can escape the pain of the hell of child loss until we are strong enough to cope with the truth of what has happened.

The death of a child is never just one loss, but rather a complexity of losses that is far too much for the mind and heart to handle all at once.

To miscarry a baby is to lose the hope of the child that was to bring so much joy into your life. There were dreams formed from the moment you learned of the miracle of your child's impending birth. With today's technology, we can see and hear our baby's heart beating very early on – a miracle in and of itself. We anticipate each day with growing joy. We name this child. We have a picture already formed in our minds what this child will look like. We envision wonderful things with our child such as the first steps, the first tooth, and the first word. We spend hours thinking about our child's personality. We daydream about our child's graduation from school. We think about our child's education, and we often begin a savings account for education the day we find out there is a baby on the way.

Our thoughts are preoccupied day and night with the coming of this beautiful miracle of life!

When a pregnancy ends too soon resulting in child loss, each dream that we had for our child is a loss, too. Our child was already a very real part of our lives, and suddenly we feel lost and abandoned. A large part of our future has been stolen away. We don't even know who we are now that our child is gone. When that little heart stops beating the void we feel is unbearable!

This is so true of any child loss – no matter what stage or age the loss may be! These feelings of emptiness and loss of a future are synonymous with child loss.

We never, ever expect a young child to die! That's so far out of the context of life that child loss isn't even on our radar. How can our human minds comprehend something of this magnitude? Our child had an eternal soul, and now that child is gone, and we are stripped of a miracle. Stripped of a future. And, it feels like we're also stripped of hope!

We cuddle babies. We center our every thought on our child's well-being. We document every milestone no matter how small or insignificant it might seem to others. The first tooth. The first time our child sits up. The first step. The first time our baby says "mama" or "dada" is all part of this magnificent journey called parenthood.

When our child's life ends, part of us ends, too.

Every day our child is with us, our relationship with our child grows deeper and more meaningful. We spend endless hours awake at night calming our child's fears, soothing our child through coughs and fevers, and being our child's advocate when our child can't speak up for himself.

We are our child's protector, caregiver, role model, nurse, teacher, counselor, security, and so much more! Our love for our child cannot be explained in here words. Our love for our child is a connection of mind, body, spirit, and soul. We are so bound by love that we can feel our child's every pain, and we live for that moment when we can share in our child's every joy.

Each day that our child lives, our love for our child deepens and intensifies!

Is it any wonder that when a child dies part of us dies, too? This is why I say child loss is not a singular loss, but rather a continuum of losses that we will experience for the remainder of our days on this earth.

Child loss is truly a heartbreak like none other and that is why we have been provided with a place called the foggy abyss – a holding place where we are protected from feeling the blunt force of too much pain all at once.

We enter this place of fog not by chance, but rather by design. Our hearts and minds cannot withstand an overload of shock and trauma. So, we have been given by design a place of protection for a while.

Living in the fog is noticeable to us – we fight hard to climb out of it, but we simply don't have the strength in the early days following the loss of our child.

Every minute in life feels strangely and noticeably weird. Every breath we take hurts. Every time our heart beats there is an inner ache screaming, "I want my child. I can't do this! I can't go on without my child. I can't do this even one more minute!"

*And, the protective fog embraces us tighter shielding us
from the full force of the storm that rages within.*

How long does this fog last following the loss of our child?
We wake up each day groggy from fighting sleep, yet needing
the gift of falling into a state of unconsciousness where there
is the absence of pain, if only for a few hours. Who can deal
with the pain of child loss every minute of the day? The pain
is far too much for us to bear. Yet, the fog keeps us in a state
of semi-consciousness and like it or not, life is pulling,
pushing, and shoving us to re-enter living again.

Only this time we must live without the joy of our child.

The internal tug-of-war between wanting to live and not
wanting to live is frightening. This struggle is something that
almost every bereaved parent has fought. We're afraid to talk
to others about this because we've never had these feelings
before. There is a pulling on us to want to go be with our
child. Yet, life on earth is pulling at us from another
direction saying, "You belong here. Your life is not yet over.
Stay. Your day of hope will come."

When we close our eyes we see our child with outstretched
arms calling us, and it is torment – this desire to go. We
know this is grief in its deepest sense causing these feelings.
Intellectually we understand that grief is the driving force
behind these thoughts, but emotionally we want so much to
reach out, grab hold of our child's hands and go.

Our love for our child is so intense that all else is shoved
aside and we have only one wish and that is to be with our
child again.

*Grief wreaks havoc on our hearts and minds. Grief
throws us into a vulnerable state and this is just one more*

reason why we need the protection and safe keeping of the foggy abyss.

Parents, siblings, and grandparents who experience this daily strife often think they are standing on the very brink of insanity. This is an emotional state that we've never felt before, and it is so frightening that we shy away from telling others how fragile we really feel. Normally, our strongest driving force in life is to live. And, now we find ourselves filled with these new feelings of wanting nothing more than to be with our child – even at the expense of leaving this earthly life.

How thankful we should be for the protection and guidance of the fog! We are literally being rescued during our darkest hours of grief and despair and we are drawn to a safe place mentally where we can escape the full punch of the pain of child loss.

Losing a child is too much heartbreak for the heart and soul to experience all at once!

Some may look at us in our foggy, robotic state and say, "She's in denial. Total denial of what has happened." Other may look at us and say, "He had a breakdown. That's why he's not understanding what happened and isn't moving on in life." Still others will say, "Look how great they're handling the death of their child! They're not even shedding a tear. How strong they are!"

All the while, inwardly we're screaming, "I'm trapped! I'm trapped in this fog and I can't see two feet in front of me. I can't think straight. I can't even remember how to get dressed! I can't figure out how to plan a meal. I can't even remember how to get from the bedroom to the couch."

And, what's worse, "I really don't care. I just want my child back."

How long does this foggy state last? This fog lasts as long as we need it to last. It could be weeks. It could be months. Or it could be a year or more. It's different for each person. No two people will ever grieve the loss of their child in the same way.

Living in the fog gives us the opportunity to learn how to breathe again – without our child. The fog slows down the hands on the clock so that we can sort out the tasks for the day. Eat breakfast. Shower. Go to work. Come home.

Little-by-little the fog loosens its grip so that we can begin to finally function enough to complete our daily routine. And, for a moment it feels good. We are finally doing some of the things we forgot how to do. We are starting life all over again. We are finding our "new normal" without even realizing it.

As the fog loosens its hold on us we being to enter a new phase on this journey we call child loss. We are slowly beginning to understand what really happened. Our child is gone. Away. Separated. Not with us. And, the harshness of those words hits us like a lightning bolt. We are suddenly filled with fear like we've never experienced before. And, we cry out in despair begging to remain in the foggy abyss for just a while longer. The acute pain of the reality of child loss is too much.

We know that we are not ready to face life without our child!

Let's pause here and try to more fully understand why this foggy place is a blessing to us. We shouldn't fear the fog, nor should we fight it. It's okay to just exist for a while – to robotically go through the motions of life. Why doctors and other clinicians don't explain this to us I'll never know!

In the first months following the death of our child we will experience every emotion known to mankind. We will be on a roller coaster every day never knowing from minute to minute what's coming. Fear. Rage. Sorrow. Panic. Anxiety. Anguish. Unrelenting pain.

Safety is found in the fog. Embrace it for as long as you need. Don't allow others to push you out of your safe harbor too soon by saying, "Get moving or you'll be stuck in grief forever." That's simply not true. We need a time for this buffer from the full brunt of pain. We're not at all stuck in grief. We're simply taking a moment to catch our breath while we're in the fog.

Deep inside you'll know when it's time to move forward. You'll know when it's time to take that critical step that moves you out of the fog into the next part of this journey of grief and loss. Step out slowly. Sure, you're afraid. But, it's a necessary next step on this pathway to finding hope – the kind of hope that will sustain you through the ongoing pain and heartbreak of child loss.

2 NO TIME FRAME

I don't know of any person who loves to live in a place of daily pain. In fact, it is now commonplace to have pain clinics in every major city in the United States and abroad. We fight hard to get rid of pain. We take pills that numb us. We do exercises that relieve pain, tension, and stress. We use biofeedback. Some even resort to acupuncture. The practice of yoga is making a big comeback as a means of stretching and relieving pain.[1]

And, let us not minimize the use of prayer when dealing with pain. When we are in deep pain, we automatically cry out to God for relief from our pain and suffering through the use of prayer. Prayer has been studied for years in major hospitals to see if there is indeed positive relief from pain by the use of prayer. Since prayer is a very subjective issue for many, the conclusions are often debated, but it cannot be dismissed that prayer works!

When dealing with the incredibly intense, ongoing internal pain from child loss, parents will go to great lengths to seek relief from this pain. I have been working in the field of grief for over twenty-five years now, and I've met thousands of parents suffering through the pain of loss. Never once have I heard a parent say, "Oh, I don't mind this pain. It's okay. I can easily live with this every day."

Just the opposite is true! As bereaved parents, we want to know one thing almost immediately after the loss of a child occurs. We want to know when the pain is going to end. When am I going to stop feeling this crushing weight of pain on my heart and mind? When? When? When? When will this horrible, indescribable pain come to an end? When will I get some relief?

If only there was an easy answer to that most difficult question! I'd love to be able to say that in six months to a year your pain will be gone. I'd love to say, "Follow these six principles, practice them daily, and you will be pain free in ninety days."

We want a quick fix to the pain of child loss. We need to know that there is an end to this suffering. But, the truth may not be what you want to hear. In fact, I know this is something that no parent of child loss wants to hear.

The truth is that the pain from child loss never ends. The pain changes, but it never totally goes away. Over time, the pain becomes less raw and is more manageable. But, there will always be an emptiness in your heart. The hole that was left when your child died will always be there. There will always be pain – always a reminder that something very precious is missing from your life. When your child died, part of your heart died, too. And, that part of your heart will always feel pain.

But, this is not a hopeless situation, by any means. Sometimes we get so bogged down in the fact that we will always feel pain that we fail to understand that over time you get to choose how to manage this pain. You get to choose how to take this pain and create a new you. Please don't take this statement to mean that the loss of your child is diminished. It simply means that the old you is gone. And, through the pain of losing a child a new you will emerge, and you do have control over what that new person will be like.

If someone had told me when I experienced my first loss that I would be able to choose how to manage my pain, I think I would have screamed out in anger saying, "You're a liar! I don't believe that this pain will ever ease. I don't believe that this pain will ever allow me to feel new or to have any kind of purpose in my life again! I don't believe I can go on living like this!"

I'm here to help guide you gently through this raw pain and to tell you that I am living proof that better, gentler days are ahead. There will be a day when your pain quiets, and a new sense of hope will emerge inside of your now broken heart.

Will you ever feel like your old self again? Absolutely not! Your old self died the moment your child died. How could you be the same when so much of your identity left the day your child died?

I am here to say that the acute pain you experience when you leave the safety of the foggy abyss will not last forever. But – and this is a big but – you must make a very conscious decision at some point along your grief journey to daily release some of the pain of loss. This is hard work. It takes a lot of effort. And, it doesn't come naturally. But, you will do it. I have no doubt about that.

This journey of grief that every bereaved parent travels following the loss of a child is a see-saw journey. Emotions are up, down, and all around never giving us time to catch our breath. No two people will grieve in exactly the same way, either. Our grief needs change from day-to-day.

Sometimes our needs change from hour-to-hour. There are times when we want to be left totally alone. Other times, we need to be surrounded by loved ones and lots of support. Still other times we will need to shout out in anger to help release some of the internal pain. And, there are moments when our greatest need will be to fall on our knees and pray.

Losing a child is one of the worst traumas we can ever experience. There are no set rules that we follow when we are trying to push our way through the pain of trauma into a place of a more manageable, peaceful life. Trauma is our emotional response to the death of our precious child that we loved with all of our heart. And, as we know, finding our way through trauma is not easy! We need help, support, time, and lots of rest along the way.

There will be many days when we feel the need to cry alone. To others this might seem unhealthy, but the truth is we each must face our grief head-on at some point. It's during those raw, unsolicited moments that we can pour out our pain from the inner depths of our heart and spew out what we are really and truly feeling without fear of any judgment from others. It's necessary to have these cleansing moments of unfiltered grief.

Too much of the time we worry about what others will think if we express what we are feeling inside. We must give ourselves permission to release our true inner feelings if we want to get to a point of healing some of this intense pain of loss.

Tears make others uncomfortable, and that makes us uncomfortable, too. Even in our grief we don't want to offend others. The truth is that most of us cannot handle seeing another person cry. We want to immediately take away the pain, fix the problem, and make life pure, wholesome, and happy again.

Isn't it a shame that we begin teaching our young children not to express themselves through tears? We say things like, "Stop being such a baby. You're a big boy now, and big boys don't cry." "If you stop crying, mommy will give you a special treat." "You make others feel so sad when you cry, and it's not nice to make others sad." We work hard to get our children to suppress their tears. Is it any wonder this same thinking carries over into adulthood?

Holding in our tears doesn't work in child loss. Tears will flow like a river. And, we will cry "the ugly cry" as Oprah Winfrey calls it. There are times when our inner moanings don't even sound human. That's how bad our pain is. And, the more we try to restrain our tears and pain, the harder the pain tries to surface until finally we are able to release some of this intense pain through our tears.

Remember – tears are healthy. Stop listening to people who tell you that tears are a sign of weakness! There should be no shame in shedding tears. Our bodies were designed to cry when we are in pain!

Child loss is not the time to try to prove to anyone our strength. We're not in a strength building contest. This is a real life journey – a grief journey – and each step forward is a slow, painful step that is accompanied by tears.

When you give yourself permission to grieve, you are also giving yourself permission to find hope and healing!

We're back to that most important question. How long will we grieve and hurt after the loss of our child? We still haven't answered that question because there is no concrete answer except to say that we will always carry an empty place within our heart that is reserved only for our child.

There is absolutely nothing or no one that can fill that special place. With every beat of our heart we will be reminded that our child is no longer here with us. That doesn't mean that we will never smile again. That doesn't mean that every second of every day for the rest of our lives we will be consumed with only grief and pain. That doesn't mean that we will never again experience any kind of joy in our lives. What it does mean is our pain will become less intense and less frequent as we travel along our personal grief journey. There will be moments of much-needed peace and tranquility in our lives when we give ourselves permission to release some of this pain.

Some parents will say, "It's been ten years and I still feel the agonizing pain of loss every day. The first thing I think about in the morning is my child, and the last thing I think about in the evening is my child. My every thought is sprinkled with thoughts of my child all day long. When will this agony of missing my child end?"

This is where I will emphasize the fact that grief is both tricky and very individual. The more we understand grief, the more we will gain the ability to manage the pain rather than allow it to fully and completely control our every thought.

Let me explain this another way. If we are suddenly placed in a very frightening situation where we are on a dark, long, winding road without a map, compass, proper clothing, food or water, we soon find out that we're in very deep trouble. But, if we're suddenly thrust onto this unknown road and we know we must find out way out in order to survive, it helps us to have a flashlight, a jacket, shoes, a blanket, protein bars, and lots of water for the treacherous journey ahead. An emergency kit, so-to-speak, is what we need for survival.

This is how it is on our journey of grief from child loss. If we don't understand even a little bit about grief and how it works, our journey is going to be a hundred times longer and far more difficult. If we don't understand that we will experience mood changes, sleeplessness, anxiety, extreme sadness, inability to focus, and frequent bouts of crying, we will think we're either going totally crazy or we've landed in an airtight hopeless situation with absolutely no way out.

On the other hand, if we have some knowledge of grief plus a group of friends who are there to support us – to hold us up when we are weary, to calm us when we are anxious, to catch our tears when they fall and blur our vision – then our journey is going to be a lot more bearable in the years to come.

Finding Support

I cannot emphasize enough the importance of surrounding yourself with a strong, ongoing support system following the loss of your child! Your support system can make all of the difference in the world as to the intensity and length of your pain!

In my dealings with thousands of bereaved parents in the past twenty-five years, I can tell you that hands down the biggest complaint of the bereaved is the fact that friends disappear soon after the death of a child leaving the parents with little to no support at all. Why do friends disappear so suddenly following the death of a child? It is my understanding that others do not like to see family or friends in pain. It is difficult to watch someone suffering and not be able to take away at least part of that pain. Also, it's emotionally and physically draining to be around others who are grieving the loss of a child. For a long time, the bereaved parents are unable to contribute anything to the bond of friendship. The drain becomes too much for friends so they quietly move on without us.

We have two choices at this point in our grief journey. We can become very angry and bitter and remain there for the rest of our lives. Or, we can seek support elsewhere to help us travel this frightening journey of loss.

"It's not fair!" we cry out. "Why should we have to reach out in our pain? Why have my friends abandoned me in my time of need?"

We must reach out in order to survive and eventually bring back some joy and purpose into our lives. Isn't this what our child would want for us? I cannot imagine any of my children wanting me to suffer intense pain all of the days of my life. In fact, I'll be so bold as to say there is no child that would want to see their parents suffer forever.

And, don't we want relief from this pain? Of course we do! If our friends have disappeared, then sadly it's up to us to find the support and help we need to get us to a better place in life emotionally.

Where do we find this support that we so desperately need once we emerge from the foggy abyss into the painful truth of the reality of our loss?

Thankfully, we live in a time when we can connect with support almost instantly if we use social media. There are many wonderful online support groups for parents, grandparents, and siblings who have experienced a loss. About twenty years ago I began an online support page, SilentGrief.com. Today, that support is still available and I urge you to go there often to find articles and other daily help for your walk through grief.

When silentgrief.com quickly grew to a readership in the thousands, I knew there needed to be extra support. So I formed an online Facebook support group: Silent Grief – Child Loss Support. Thousands of bereaved parents and grandparents from around the world now visit daily seeking and receiving help and support.

There are also child loss websites and blogs where you can connect with other parents, grandparents, and family members. Please use the blog SilentGriefSupport.com frequently as another one of your resources for help.

There are many, many great books available in every format – all affordable to anyone. Please visit Amazon.com and search for child loss books. Read the reviews and choose books that you feel would be helpful to you. I'm so pleased to say that a book I authored more than twenty years ago, *Silent Grief*, is one the few books on child loss that remains in the top 100 best books on child loss for over twenty years. *Silent Grief* is truly a timeless classic and it will give you much-needed insights into the world of grief, hope, and healing for child loss.

I highly recommend any books by Elisabeth Kubler-Ross, the woman who literally brought the word "grief" to the forefront and has made it a household word. How very thankful we are for her hard work in helping the world understand the depth of pain brought on by child loss.

I also strongly urge you to find a local support group to meet with in your community. A lot of our cities have active chapters of The Compassionate Friends – a wonderful support group. Check with your local hospital, chaplain, or pastor to ask where you can find a support group in your community. Meeting face-to-face with bereaved parents will give you a community of friends that will remain by your side forevermore.

Lastly, seek grief counseling if you are experiencing depression, suicidal thoughts, or if you feel you no longer can function. Sometimes spending a few months in one-on-one counseling can bring you through the dark tunnel of hopelessness to a place where you are ready to take the next brave step in this journey of loss.

Why have I spent so much time giving you resources and ways to find support? Because support is the most critical factor in your grief walk. This is one time you must not try to get through the pain alone! If you have a supportive, caring family, group of friends, church family, and co-workers, then you are among the very blessed. But, even with that much support, I strongly urge you to seek out some of these additional resources mentioned.

You can never have too much support when it comes to working through the pain and grief of child loss. In order to get to a healthy place of hope, you absolutely must have the help of others. Do not try to travel this grief journey alone!

3 AM I GOING CRAZY?

It's difficult to know what to include in a book that is of great importance such as this, so I have prayed many, many hours for wisdom to know just what to include that will help you. This particular chapter made the cut for two reasons. Almost every parent who has lost a child feels like they are literally going crazy at some point during the grief journey. And, sadly, this is an emotional state that is very seldom talked about. So, I have decided to address this issue of deep concern and despair.

The first time I experienced loss was an early miscarriage. This was during a time when people didn't talk openly about miscarriages. In fact, I had no clue what a miscarriage was, nor did my doctor explain the possibility to me. I remember being given a pamphlet during my first obstetrical visit, and in that pamphlet was a brief paragraph stating that if you experience bleeding of any kind during your pregnancy, call your doctor or go to the nearest hospital.

That was the extent of information I had at the time my bleeding began. For more details about the physical changes that take place during a loss by miscarriage I encourage you to get a copy of my book *Silent Grief*. In this particular chapter we'll focus on the emotional changes that take place during loss rather than going into the facts about how a miscarriage affects the physical body.

I remember feeling scared – *petrified* is a better word – when I miscarried. I experienced emotions I had never felt before. I cried at the drop of a pin. I was jealous of others with babies. I had emotions of guilt, feeling as though I had done something wrong that made me lose my baby. I felt like life's biggest failure for not keeping my precious baby safe.

My thoughts were jumbled and out of control. Life no longer made sense to me. Life felt wrong and all mixed up. I thought that good things happened to good people and something terribly bad had just happened to me, so I concluded that I must be a bad person – a very, very bad person. My heart felt heavy and so full of discouragement.

I felt abandoned. Alone. Empty. Lost.

To put it another way, I was angry at life!

And, I was angry with God, but so afraid to say that aloud.

Life was spinning out of control and it was the most afraid I had ever been. I thought for sure that I was going crazy!

What I did not know then that I now know is the emotions I was experiencing were far from crazy. Every parent who loses a child – whether early on or much later – experiences a similar range of emotions and will at some point question his or her own sanity.

CLARA HINTON

How I wish someone had explained this to me! So much additional grief would have been spared if only I knew that these emotions were a normal part of my grief journey!

More recently, I have had another tragic loss in my life – the loss of an adult son. And, I have once again been touched by all of the emotions I've mentioned plus some new ones. Night terrors. Hearing my son's voice when I am driving in the car or alone at night. Feeling my son's arm brush up against me. These are all things that previously would have made me think I was losing my mind. I now know better. I understand more completely how grief and trauma from loss affect us, and I'm not as frightened as I was in the past with my previous loss. I'm sharing these things with you because I don't want you to be frightened of these new emotions.

When we are experiencing deep, traumatic grief, we do not always think clearly. We already know that for a long time we live in a semi state of denial known as the grief fog. After the fog begins to lift, we feel a new kind of pain. I call it a tormenting, teasing pain. It's a pain that tugs at our heartstrings and plays with our emotions on every level.

"Did my child really die?" "There must have been some mistake. That wasn't my child they brought to the hospital." "I heard him calling to me during the night. I need to find him and help him. He's lost." "I know I just saw my daughter walking in that crowd of people. I tried to run up to her and get her to come home, but she got away."

These thoughts and visions are not at all uncommon to the parent who has lost a child. For a very long time we will question whether or not our child really died. Yes, we do understand our child's death intellectually. But emotionally we cannot yet believe it's true. And, so begins this tug-of-war within that makes us feel like we are truly losing our sanity.

It's not uncommon to experience full blown nightmares for a while – the kind where we wake up drenched in sweat and we're screaming. This is all part of the trauma – part of preparing our minds to get to a point where we are no longer buffered from the reality of what has happened.

Are we going crazy? Not at all! A broken heart is a heavy load to carry!

There are many moments when our anxiety will grow out of control and our thoughts run wild with fear. We want only one thing to comfort us and that is our child. Nothing anyone says or does helps. We spend countless hours crying. We will often get in the car and begin driving to nowhere in particular just to get away to a place where we can scream and not be heard by others.

These moments are all necessary in order to release some of the built up pain and pressure from the grief we are holding inside. There are moments when the grief builds up to a point where we believe that we will not make it one minute longer. We've reached our breaking point.

When you get to this point in your grief it's time to stop. Back away, and take a long, deep cleansing breath. Repeat ten times. Then affirm, "I am not alone. I can make it through five more minutes." Continue repeating that affirmation until your breathing becomes more regular and your panic begins to ease.

As you practice this healing exercise your pulse will calm and you will begin to gain a bit of control. Child loss leaves us feeling so totally out of control that we must remind ourselves often that life still matters and there are still "constants" in life. Every day the sun rises and the sun sets – a very basic principle that can bring us relief when we feel like we're teetering on the very brink of insanity.

It's critically important for us to know and understand ways of calming our grief!

Let's shift gears for a minute and talk about something else that is rarely mentioned to bereaved parents. Sometimes the way we choose to grieve will cause others to think we have lost our minds.

Let that sentence sink in for a minute. There are times that the way we "choose to grieve" will cause others to think we've lost our minds!

Can you relate to that? I know that I can!

We are all familiar with the phrase "the empty chair at the table" referencing the empty place left by our child who has now died. There are some parents who choose to set a place for their child at the table. This is a comfort to them – a way of remembering and including their child in daily life.

Others might bake a cake on their child's birthday and throw a party, including purchasing and wrapping gifts for their child. Some parents choose to decorate their child's grave site with toys or something that was meaningful to them and their child.

I have known several parents who have brought sleeping bags and slept on their child's grave site on different occasions. Some choose to wear their child's ashes in a locket around their neck. Others choose to leave their child's bedroom intact – dirty socks still on the floor, bed unmade, towel hanging on the bed post. Still others choose to lock the child's bedroom door and never again enter the room.

We all have those well-meaning friends who watch us from afar as we try to find our own special way to express our grief, and they will often say, "She went crazy. I've never seen such behavior."

Worse yet are the friends who feel they must come directly to you and tell you that you're crazy. That's the very last thing in the world we need to hear at our most vulnerable moments in grief.

I feel the need to shout this message to the world:

"There is no right or wrong way to grieve the loss of a child! A parent must have permission to grieve in his or her own way and in his or her own time! Stop trying to tell them they must conform to your ways!"

If there is only one message that you take away from this chapter, I hope you will remember that one basic truth. Every person must have permission and space to grieve the loss of their child in his or her own way without judgment. Write that down on paper. Place it where you can read it several times every day. Why? Because there will be many moments on this grief journey when you will begin to doubt yourself and that kind of self-doubt only compounds your grief.

Do whatever brings a bit of comfort to you. If you want to wallpaper your room with your child's photo because that brings you a bit of comfort, then do it. Follow your heart and not the criticisms that others may throw your way.

If you want to visit your child's grave site and spend an hour or more talking to your child because it calms your fears and makes your child feel near, then talk to your child without hesitation. You don't need permission from others to grieve in your own way. You only need to give yourself permission to freely grieve.

There are absolutely no set rules or standards for how you should or should not grieve the loss of your child. Just because you express your grief differently from another does not mean you have lost either your intelligence or your insanity.

Follow your heart and grieve in whatever way is best for you!

Not everyone will understand your way of grief, but not everyone has to understand. They are not the ones carrying the pain of losing your child and living with a broken heart.

Please remind yourself every day many times over the way you grieve is always going to be unique to you. There is no right or wrong way to grieve. Your job is to find what works best for you.

4 I CAN'T DO THIS – BUT I HAVE TO!

There comes a point in our grief soon after we leave the foggy abyss and the protection it gave us when we seem to crumble and cry out, "I can't do this anymore! I can't go on another day without my child! I don't have the strength to do this one day more!"

Have you been there? Have you cried those words of pain and despair? I know I have said those words many times through sobs and tears. The energy and strength to keep going on is depleted. The pain is too much. We feel weak, lost, and so alone without our child. We feel depleted and, even worse, we feel defeated!

To lose a child is to lose a large part of ourselves, too. We invest so much time, energy, and love into our child that often when a child dies we don't know who we are anymore. Loss of identity is a huge part of child loss!

We were there when our child was born and we had so many hopes and dreams for our child. In fact, as parents we probably spent thousands of hours daydreaming about the future with our child even before he or she was born. We spent hours dreaming about where our child will go to school, what vocation our child will choose, and where our child will live when he or she becomes an adult. We daydream about college, graduations, birthday parties, trips, family vacations, weddings, and grandchildren. The majority of our thoughts center on our child.

We share these dreams with others. We often journal about our hopes and dreams for our child. Thoughts of our child literally consume us. Why? Because that's how intense a parent's love is for their child. I firmly believe a parent and child have a very real heart and soul connection that begins the very moment of conception. And, when a child leaves this earth, our hearts go through a major shock transformation. With the blink of an eye so much of our life is wiped out!

Losing a child is devastation and the pain is so deep and intense that we experience many, many moments when we truly want to give up. Life is just too hard to go on living without our child!

Please take the time to go back to Chapter 2 and read again about the importance of having a strong support system in place to help you. When we feel too weary to carry on in life, we must call in the troops, so-to-speak, to come alongside of us and carry our weak, weary souls until we are able to receive some much-needed life-giving replenishment.

These moments of wanting to give up are the times when we lean heavily on others to hold us up and walk us through those dark, difficult days when our mind is screaming, "I can't do this! I just can't live this life any more without my child. It hurts too badly to go on!"

Sadly, there are few people who understand this desert we have entered and many will begin to tell us to stop living in the past. They don't understand the way grief works on our minds, bodies, and souls, and many friends will abandon us at this point, because quite truthfully life has gone on for them and our despair is now beginning to drag them down. Very few people have friends willing to stand by them during these months of agony and despair.

What a terrible roller coaster ride this is! We feel so lost and so misunderstood. It feels as though we are lost at sea in the midst of a raging storm without the captain of our ship.

Here is where our grief becomes very complex and multi-dimensional. We're at a critical crossroads of not wanting to live without our child (the result of cumulative months of overwhelming, relentless grief) and knowing that we must go on. Life on this earth is precious and full of God-given purpose. At this point, we must face our grief head-on and try our best to prepare for our reentry into life.

This is a real life battlefield that so many who grieve the loss of a child are afraid to talk about for fear of judgment, further abandonment, and more isolation. Isn't it a shame that we have to hide our true feelings for fear of being judged? Isn't it sad that we can't be our true selves to others for fear that our few friends will also leave us stranded on this island of grief? How blessed are those who have friends who provide listening ears and a shoulder to fall on when we are in such a pit of grief!

There will be moments in your grief journey when you entertain the thought of dying so that you can be with your child. The pain described in Chapter 1 has now become so overwhelming that it scares the life out of us! Living all the remainder of our days on earth without our child can become a thought that is too overwhelming for us.

Please pay close attention here. If you are having suicidal thoughts you must seek help! To want to be with your child is a normal thought, but to think about ways of ending your time on this earth is a critical thought that sends signals out that you need help right away. Do not delay! Your community has a crisis hotline for help. Keep it handy and call.

Or, you can call the **National Suicide Prevention Lifeline at 1-800-273-TALK.** The National Suicide Prevention Lifeline is the United States based suicide prevention network of 161 crisis centers that provides a 24-hour, toll free hotline available to anyone in suicidal crisis or emotional distress. After dialing **1-800-273-TALK (8255),** you will be routed to your nearest crisis center to receive immediate counseling and local mental health referrals.

Death for those left behind following child loss is not an option! Why? Because we have the rest of our lives to live!

Pause. Take a deep breath. Drink a glass of water if you need to divert your attention and get your thoughts together. Keep reading this affirmation over and over again. Read it a thousand times if you have to. Read it until it sinks in and you really believe it.

Death for those left behind is not an option! Why? Because we have the rest of our lives to live!

Note: If you cannot shake these feelings of resisting moving forward in your life, please take this seriously and seek the help of a professional counselor. There are many well-established grief counselors available who can help you begin to change your thinking and point you in the direction of learning to live life without your child. Is this easy? Absolutely not!

But, life is our only choice! Counselors are trained professionals who can give us direction and help.

When we say, "I can't go on," it means the daily grief is too hard and too painful to bear by ourselves. So, how do we find the energy and the desire to go on following the loss of our child? This desire does not come all at once. Far from it! There is a very slow emergence back into doing some of the daily life routines that will begin to push us forward in our grief walk.

I can remember in my early months following my stillborn son, Samuel, not wanting to move off of the couch. It was all I could do to move from the bed to the couch, then back to bed again. It often took an entire day of battling in my mind trying to convince myself to get a shower. And, when I finally did shower, I fell to the couch totally exhausted. Grief had entered my mind and body and taken residence there.

Grief is so exhausting! It totally zaps our energy leaving us feeling like we can't move.

One of the things that helped me was knowing I had others who depended on me. I would lay on the couch, head buried in my pillow soaked in tears for hours at a time. In the distance, I could hear a child of mine saying, "Mom, are you okay?" and those words pierced me clear to my soul, yet also helped push me inch-by-inch, breath-by-breath out of my paralyzing despair.

It is so important for those in deep grief to know that they are needed and are important to others! That's one more reason it's so vital to have a strong support system in place where others can help pull us gently back into the flow of life again.

This emergence from the total consumption of grief into a place of knowing we must go on doesn't happen overnight. How long does it take? Nobody can answer that question because it's so different for each person. For me, it took the better part of six months to gain back the energy and the desire to get out of bed, eat a bit of breakfast, get a shower, and clear off the kitchen table. When I was able to do that much I knew progress was being made.

Many grieving parents must get back to work very quickly after the death of their child, and this is something that always concerns me. Three to five days off of work is not even time to digest what has happened, let alone give a parent the opportunity to begin processing the shock and trauma of losing their child. Yet, most parents do not have the blessing of taking an extended leave of absence from work. This is a pet peeve of mine, and I will continue to work very hard to educate employers and our legislators about how important it is to give a parent time to grieve and come to a better understanding of what resources are needed to get through this trauma of losing a child.

If you are forced to get back to work and some kind of daily routine right after the loss of your child, please heed this caution. If you push away all of your grief and shove it to the back burner of your heart, the grief will eventually turn into a blazing, roaring fire of uncontrollable emotions and will immobilize you. We must work through grief daily once we push through the protection of the fog or the emotions of grief will snowball and eventually plow us over.

One day, one step at a time is the best way to work through the grief of child loss.

Why do we have to re-enter life after loss? Because we have others who need us. Because we are among the living. Because we love ourselves enough to join life once again.

Will it ever be the same? No, we will never view life the same as we did before our child died, but that doesn't mean that we can never enjoy a smile or a walk through a meadow or soak up the beauty of a sunrise over the majestic ocean. It just means that we will see things differently – on a higher level – than we did before our child died.

Many parents will say, "No! I can't do that! I'll never be able to smile again! I'll never be able to live life with any amount of joy again!" That is a common thought and is closely tied to the emotional turmoil and emotional conflict we are experiencing. Please understand that moving towards reentry into life does not mean you will be your old self again. The moment your child died you became a different person. Part of your heart was whisked away. You can never go back to being the old you again. But, you can learn ways of living life again.

This progression back to life means learning how to love again. If you stop and truly evaluate your thoughts there is probably a lot of anger and guilt that you didn't have before your child died. You are angry at life for taking your child. You are angry for the circumstances that caused your child's death. You are angry that your solemn prayers didn't protect your child from death. You are angry that your child was taken from you!

And, the burden of guilt is a heavy load that now abides in you and weighs you down pressing you from every side. You feel guilty because you couldn't save your child from death. You feel guilty for the times you lost your patience with your child. You feel guilty for not spending enough time with your child. You feel guilty for not doing more to protect your child. You feel guilty for complaining about your child. You feel guilty because you believe you failed your child.

On top of being angry and guilty, we're scared beyond words! We're so afraid of facing the future without our child.

When we are filled with anger, guilt, and fear it's impossible to love ourselves. And, when we don't love ourselves, we become caught up in the idea that we don't deserve to live. We feel that we don't deserve to be happy. We think we're not worthy of being loved by anyone. We fall into a vicious cycle of self-hatred and total disappointment in ourselves. Because we did not prevent our child's death, we do not have the love we need for ourselves. Until we love ourselves again, we cannot forgive ourselves.

At some point along this grief journey, we must learn how to forgive ourselves and to love ourselves. And, only then can we dismantle enough of this inner, gnawing pain to be able to say, "I didn't think I could do this, but I have to!" "I have to work hard to find a way to enter back into life again!"

Moving forward in life without our child is the hardest thing we will ever have to do. But, we must find a way to move beyond the paralyzing fear and immobilizing anger and guilt or we will never regain the ability to love again.

Try this for the next ninety days and you will begin to see a very noticeable shift in the way you view the new you. No, your pain will not disappear, but if you promise to do this exercise I can guarantee you that some of the weight of your grief will be lifted.

Get some note cards and write down the following:

"I release all anger inside of me and think only of peace. I forgive myself and let go of all feelings of guilt, because I am worthy of love."

Place the note cards wherever you can see them first thing in the morning, at noon, and before bed. Force yourself to read these cards and really "feel" what you are reading.

If you faithfully do this for ninety days, I guarantee you will be able to say, "I choose to move forward in life," and you will really mean it. Giving up on life is no longer an option for you!

You have just taken a big, giant step towards that place called hope.

5 THE HARDEST PART

There is nothing easy about losing a child. You can have the strongest faith there is to be found, you can have the most positive outlook on life, but when child loss hits, it will floor you and shake you to the very core of your inner being. Why? Because when such a heartbreak occurs, we are immediately thrown into a state of shock and trauma as previously discussed. Nothing makes sense in life any more, and one of the first things we begin to question is our faith – our core beliefs.

When we are faced with pain, one of the most important questions we want to have answered is "What will be the hardest part?" We want to prepare for the storm ahead, and rightly so. In child loss, we can never be what I would call "prepared." Even when we know that death is inevitable for our child due to an ongoing chronic illness, we're never prepared to say good-bye to our child. Saying good-bye is too far out of the realm of normal to even allow that to be part of our thought process. Parents are never supposed to bury their children!

It helps so much to understand more in depth about grief. When we understand what is happening to us, we can at least have a small amount of control in this life situation that feels so totally out of control.

What is the hardest part of child loss? In my talking with literally thousands upon thousands of bereaved parents over the past twenty-five years coupled with my own personal experiences with child loss, I believe the absolute hardest part is when we are faced with the fact that our child truly is gone from this earth. The hardest part is when we reach that critical moment of understanding that this is forever. There is no turning back. Nothing we can say or do will change the outcome of what happened. No amount of prayers can return our child to us. No amount of begging and bargaining with God can change the fact that our child died.

The hardest part of child loss is that moment when our intelligence and emotions meet and understand – really understand – the finality of the loss.

This is the point when the dam breaks and the flood of sorrow sweeps over us and knocks us down again and again. We feel like we can't breathe. We feel like the world has crashed – exploded before our very eyes. We feel at war with ourselves and with God. We feel like running away and never coming back.

When we understand the hardest part – the reality of child loss – we feel like our own life has ended, too.

The hardest part of child loss is not just a fleeting moment in time. The hardest part is knowing for certain that we will never see our beautiful child's face again. We will never be able to touch our child. We will never be able to hold our child close. We will never again hear our child's voice. We will never be able to interact with our child ever again – not in this life. And, that knowledge – that reckoning with terms – is both terrifying and heartbreaking.

There is an internal shift that takes place within us when we grasp the understanding of the finality of our loss. Prior to this we were protected by the fog. Then we moved to a place where our child's death seemed real, but if we're honest, we still held out a bit of hope that somehow this was all a big mistake. A bad dream, if you will. We knew our child's death took place, but we didn't believe it.

A very real personal example I can share with you is when I delivered my stillborn son, Samuel. I never got to hear his cry, but I did get to hold him and cradle him next to my breast. I counted his little fingers and toes. I kissed his precious face over and over again. I stared at him and was in awe at what a beautiful, perfect child he was.

While holding him in my arms, I thought several times that I saw his chest moving – as though he was breathing. Intellectually, I knew he had no life in him, but I couldn't fully believe that. I didn't want to believe that! Months later my body that was no longer pregnant still felt pregnant to me. I knew my baby was no longer inside of me, but…I had not yet reached that hardest part of grief where I fully understood – fully believed – that my baby Samuel was born that that I said hello and good-bye to him all in the same day.

He was gone forever, yet everything inside of me still held out hope that this wasn't true!

I often woke up in bed and knew with certainty that I felt Samuel inside of me kicking. I would lay my hands on my tummy and actually convince myself that I felt movements. Many times I would pull up my shirt and watch my stomach moving – fully believing I saw movement and felt Samuel inside of me. I can't count the times I woke up "forgetting" that Samuel had died.

I remember very clearly my hardest day of grief. I was driving home in a thunderstorm and I was crying because I was so sad and lost not knowing how to get through the loss of my baby. I kept crying out to God to give Samuel back to me when suddenly that defining moment of truth arrived.

It was as though a lightning bolt from the storm hit me. I pulled over to the side of the road and stopped the car screaming out, "No! No! No! Please, God, no!" I screamed until I had no voice left. I had trouble breathing. My eyes were tiny slits – swollen from so many tears falling rapidly from my eyes.

That was the moment of my hardest part. That was the moment death became real.

I now knew with absolute certainty that my son had died. I now understood he was never coming back. I knew I would never see his face or hold his precious little body again. I finally had arrived at the hardest part – understanding the reality of my loss. There was no more denying the fact that my child had died. And, that broke my heart in two.

This is how you will come to experience the hardest part of child loss, too. You will reach that moment when all time stands till and you will know with absolute certainty that there is no turning back. You will clearly understand that your child has died.

You will have reached your hardest part of child loss when you can say, "My child has died," and you finally believe it. That's when your heart will crumble into a million pieces never to be the same again. That's when you will understand the finality of losing a child.

As mentioned before, this belief and realization of the finality of loss is a critical point in your grief walk. Many will say this is like taking ten steps backwards. The pain of loss returns with a vengeance – not that it ever left. The pain simply intensifies once you understand the reality of the loss.

Do you now understand why I called the foggy abyss somewhat of a frozen, numb state of mind where we were protected? Now, we must face the raw pain of child loss and it is terrifying. The pain is like nothing we've ever felt before!

How long does this pain of the hardest part last? There is no definite answer to the question because the grief of child loss is different for everyone. No two people will grieve the loss of their child in the same way. Please note that this is where a parent can unknowingly, unintentionally get stuck in deep, inconsolable grief. I strongly urge everyone to call on that support system that we talked about before. Because you now understand without one shred of doubt that your child is not coming back, the pain of loss is often immobilizing at this point. This is the critical crossroads where parents feel as though they are teetering between life and death themselves.

Many emotions rise to the surface again, the main ones being fear, anger, and a sense of overall loss of everything meaningful in life. There is the fear of facing the unknown future without your child. There is the fear of something terrible happening again. There is the fear of trusting in life. Our minds work overtime thinking that if this tragedy can happen once, then it surely can happen again. We have suddenly lost all security in this life that we ever had!

In this shifting of emotions, we might also begin to feel an intensely growing anger that we didn't have before. This anger swells up inside of us and grows so big that we can't think straight. We are so angry that our child was taken. We are angry because life has continued on for those around us. People seldom mention our child's name any more and that angers us. We are angry at the unfairness of life. We are angry that our child was the one taken – not that we would ever wish this on anyone – but we're so angry because this was our child!

We demand answers to questions we know can never be answered. We ask, "Why me?" a million times over and we know we'll never get an answer – at least not an answer that will seem right. We ask why there is so much suffering in this world. We ask when this pain will end. We ask where the fairness is in life. We ask why we are being punished.

We ask and we demand to know why innocent children die!

And, then comes something that we never expected. We have feelings about our child's death that we're too afraid to share with anyone. These feelings scare us. We feel ashamed of ourselves for thinking such thoughts. We've never heard anyone discuss this before. Yet…we think about it all of the time.

We are angry at our child! We are very angry at our child for leaving us. That was not supposed to happen. Our child wasn't supposed to leave – not now, not this soon. Not ever!

We feel like life is one big heaping mess of loss and emptiness and we envision all of our tomorrows as empty shells. The meaningful part of life is now gone. We throw our hands up in despair, as we fall to our knees in tears. We're broken in a way that nobody can fix. And, now we understand the full meaning of child loss.

We have reached the hardest part – the part that seems like all hope is gone.

These are hard words to read, and even harder words to live. On a scale of one to ten our pain level is a twenty. We now feel the open, raw pain of child loss and we're not sure that we can make it.

Please know that his hardest part is just that – it really is the hardest part. You've been on a journey since the moment your child died, and the journey has been hard. It was somewhat sheltered during the first few months, but you have finally reached that all-time climactic point in the journey where you want to quit.

But, you know that quitting is not an option. As hard as it is to understand and grasp at this point in your journey of loss, there is still life to be lived beyond the loss of your child. I know – I truly know – how hard that is to believe. Harder yet is to accept that fact. I've personally struggled with this for a long time. But, I know it's true. As crushing and devastating as child loss is, there is still meaning and purpose in living.

When will you find that beauty? Will you ever find purpose again? I don't know when you will see beauty in your life again. That's personal. It takes some parents of child loss many years before they can begin to see any beauty in life. For others, it might be a year or two. But, eventually you will emerge from this raw pain, and the pain of reality will begin to dull enough that you will see some light begin to emerge from this deep, dark place of grief.

You will also begin to figure out your new identity and purpose in life. Will that be easy? Absolutely not! But, it will eventually happen. Your anger and inner rage will begin to diminish. Your questions will become less intense. You will begin to see life through different eyes. You will begin to find a reason to live, and as you do you will notice that your open wounds will begin to form a scar.

What happens to your close relationships? How do marriages handle all of this stress and pain? What about the siblings left behind? What about grandparents?

Because these questions are so important I will address them in the next chapter. They deserve specific attention.

Before closing this chapter, though, I'd like to say that many parents are plagued during this part of grief – the part when you realize that your child is really and truly gone – by an inner gnawing that you must forgive everyone around you. In fact, we are often pounded with the idea that you must "forgive and forget" in order to heal.

Let me interject here that I believe in forgiveness. But, I also know that this is not the time to think about forgiveness if your child's life was taken by a drunk driver. When you are in the midst of your own personal trauma, please don't force the issue of forgiveness on yourself right now. It's too much!

If your child died at the hand of a murderer, please don't think you must get to the jail and face the murderer eye-to-eye and say, "I forgive you." You are too weak and too torn emotionally to work through the choice of forgiveness at this time in your grief.

If you were the parent who ran over your child accidentally with a car, or walked inside while your child drowned in the swimming pool, it will be important for you to forgive yourself, but please don't beat yourself up over this right now. You've got enough pain to deal with already, and learning to forgive is a very long, complicated process. Don't burden your heart with more pain just yet.

If your child's life ended by suicide, you are full of guilt for not recognizing the signs. It will be very important for you to forgive yourself because you're going to self-blame. Please don't add guilt to guilt right now. In time, when your grief is less hard, visit SAVE.org – Suicide Awareness Voices of Education. *Suicide: Survivors* is a wonderful book published on suicide and suicide grief. The author, Adina Wrobleski, was the original founder of SAVE and an expert on suicide. She has spent many years studying the subject after her daughter, Lynn, died by suicide in the late 1970's. Reading this book is a good "first step" for a parent trying to work through the difficult journey of understanding more about suicide and the importance of forgiving yourself for being a survivor.

For now – during this hardest part of living through the torment of the reality of child loss – be gentle on yourself. Seek support. You'll need lots of it. Get plenty of rest because your mind and body are going through tremendous pain and stress due to trauma. Be sure to express your grief. Remind yourself again and again that tears were given to us as a means of expelling and releasing some of our pain. Don't be afraid to cry!

Finally, remind yourself that this deep, raw pain will not last forever. There is hope!

6 WHAT IS HAPPENING TO OUR FAMILY?

As we know, the loss of a child doesn't just affect the heart of a mother. This is a loss that is a very complex, very multi-dimensional grief. Child loss is both a personal loss and a family loss.

It's never easy to explain this part of child loss because there are so many variables, but we will talk here about the differences in the way a mom and dad will grieve the loss of their child. We will discuss what sibling loss means and how a brother or sister will grieve the loss. And, we will also discuss the way child loss affects grandparents. I'm not at all saying these are the only members in a family that are touched by the loss of a child, but these are the ones we'll be discussing in this chapter. In all actuality, a family's response to the loss of a child could be an entire book on its own because the grief is so intertwined and complex.

When a child dies, there is almost always a breakdown in communication within a family. If we're being honest, the majority of families already have a hard time communicating among themselves. Very few families enjoy any kind of daily meal together where all are gathered around the same table to discuss how each other's day went. That type of setting has become less of a norm and is now a thing of the past due to so many hectic work and school schedules and extracurricular activities. Add to that the impact social media has had on our lives and you can easily begin to understand how, when, and why communication within the family unit is greatly on the decline.

Most people in general have lost the art of knowing how to carry on a conversation with one another. Our cell phones – mainly text messaging – have taken over the way we communicate. Rare is the family that sits down at the table to enjoy a meal together, talk about the events of the day, and then express their emotional state – happy, sad, angry, or frustrated. If we do eat a meal together we're usually on our phones checking emails, messages, or catching up with all of the news on Facebook.

I truly believe that the inability to communicate is responsible for such a high rate of divorce following the loss of a child. Data varies, but it's safe to say that every one out of four couples that eventually divorce attribute the divorce the loss of a child according to an extensive survey conducted by The Compassionate Friends in 1999.[2]

Men and women grieve very differently, and no two people will grieve the same loss in the same way. This fact poses a great deal of stress among couples in the family unit. Great detail is given in the book *Silent Grief* about these differences in the way couples grieve. If you are having and extremely difficult time within your marriage, I highly recommend getting a copy of the book to help you sort out issues of concern with a lack of communication. We will not go into deep detail here but will mention the highlights of major concern.

One of the hardest things for couples who are enduring the pain of child loss is the fact that each person is grieving the loss but neither knows how to respond to the emotional needs of the other. Both are under extreme stress and that adds more emotional confusion and pain to the mix.

Women, by nature, are more open than men with expressing their feelings – especially with other women. They cry more easily than men mostly because tears from a woman are more acceptable by society. Women also need a sense of community – a way to openly vent, share, and connect with other women. It becomes extremely difficult for couples who are both grieving the loss of their child, but they are grieving in very different ways. A mother will most often look to her husband for support and a strong shoulder to cry on during her months of distress. Her emotions are all over the place as can be expected. She is a changed person now due to such devastating heartbreak. Often the simplest of tasks have become impossible for her to do because of the immobilizing grief she's experiencing. So, she looks to her husband to be her strength and shield during her times of deep need.

She also wants and expects her husband to talk to her – to talk about their child, to talk about their pain, and to talk about their future together without their child. She wants her husband to wrap his strong arms around her and promise her that things are going to be okay.

Step back for just a moment and imagine what this does to a relationship – especially a relationship that was already having trouble communicating. Talking about something as heartbreaking as the death of their child under the best of circumstances would be a strain, and that's putting it mildly! The pressure the father feels during these moments is impossible to explain in just a few brief words. He feels lost in his own grief but is expected to be strong when inside he's falling apart.

What's really happening to the father of the child that has died? How does he express his grief? Where does he go to find support and comfort? How is he holding up under such pressure within the home? Men are fixers by nature, and that's how they love being seen by others. They are the ones who take something broken and repair it. They are the ones who figure out solutions to problems. However, we all know there is no way to repair the pain of child loss. There is no way for a father to take the ongoing, agonizing pain of loss away from those around him. He knows that, and it places such a feeling of failure on his already broken heart.

To add to this mounting burden that a father is now feeling, there is the guilt and shame he feels for not protecting his child – for not saving his child from death. He feels like he has abandoned his child and has let so many people down. Intellectually we know that's not true, but emotionally that's how he feels. Plus, the father is suffering his own pain of loss, and that adds an entirely new dimension of complexity to the way a family grieves the loss of a child.

A father will often steer clear of talking about the death of his child. It's far too uncomfortable for him. Most men don't easily share such deep emotions with others, including their partners.

Instead, a man will often spend endless hours in the garage building cabinets or shelves or a bird house. He will take hours to design an outdoor project, and a large part of his grief therapy will be to focus on making something tangible – something he can see. In the meantime, his wife, who is in deep need of being held and comforted and having someone to talk with, misinterprets her husband's absence to mean he doesn't care.

And so begins the cycle of grief miscommunication within the family unit.

Add to this the fact that when we are in deep, inconsolable pain we are often physically, emotionally, and spiritually depleted. We are in no condition to provide support, encouragement, and comfort to another when our own needs are so great. *An empty, broken heart does not have the ability to replenish another empty, broken heart.*

What is a family to do when faced with this type of situation? Some kind of intervention is critical for most couples at this time when all lines of communication are breaking down. This is especially true if their relationship was already on shaky ground prior to the loss of their child. Without the third party guidance of a trained marriage professional, pastor, or grief counselor it's easy for a relationship to crumble when a communication breakdown such as this occurs.

If you recall in previous chapters we talked about the many ways grief affects us individually. Losing a child definitely changes us in many different ways. We are exhausted due to the strain of grief. Fear is a constant companion. We can suffer physical symptoms such as nightmares and panic attacks. Our moods fluctuate from minute to minute. Our very personalities change! Aside from all of these changes, there is also a new problem that enters the lives of a husband and wife following the loss of a child. Blame. As humans, we want to blame someone or something for our child's death. This is a natural response to the pain. We feel we must find a reason this death occurred so we begin playing the blame game. And, this blaming often begins at home.

"If you had been a better father or mother she never would have started using drugs." "If you hadn't given him the car keys during the ice storm, the accident would never have happened." "If you had taken her to the doctor sooner, this death could have been prevented. You knew she was sick.

Why didn't you do something?" "If you hadn't had that argument with him, he wouldn't have taken the pills."

Do you see how easy it is to blame? We lash out at the other person because we're in such pain and we feel the need to hurt them, too. The problem is once these words spew from our mouths, there is no taking them back. Those words of blame are like an arrow to the heart that is already bleeding from brokenness.

It is my recommendation that at the very minimum couples seek some short-term grief counseling following the death of a child. This pain is too hard and too complex to work through without some guided help. When early help is accessed couples can come to a place of understanding the differences in the way they grieve and will be taught how to give each other the space needed in the early months of grief. Plus, they will learn how to communicate – really talk – to each other. This is something that will help them all throughout the days of their marriage. Another huge plus is that when a couple seeks help and comes up with a plan for their relationship to endure through this crisis their relationship often ends up stronger because now they understand and appreciate each other's individual pain and can respect, rather than tear down, each other.

When there are other children in the family, the grief of child loss gets even more complicated. While mom and dad are struggling to come to grips with the pain and many changes brought about by the death of a child, the needs of the siblings often go unnoticed – not intentionally – but because mom and dad are struggling so hard in their own world of grief.

When a child dies, siblings are lost, afraid, and so very confused, especially if the sibling is older than around age four. Under age four the child will sense emotional trauma in the home, but is too young to be able to label feelings of isolation, fear, loneliness, abandonment, and grief. For those older children, though, they are experiencing a deep loss, and they see changes happening in their parents and in their home life that are frightening. Mom cries a lot now, and her moods are unpredictable for no known reason. Stress is way out of control, and a child may hear excessive arguing coming from his parents. Dad often stays away from home more and more, and the child often feels that he or she is the one to blame for all of this.

I can remember so well the months following the sudden death of my thirteen-year-old sister. My parents' lives crumbled right before my very eyes. I was fifteen and nobody sat down with me to explain anything about death. I knew my sister died and I knew I missed her more than life. I would often lay in my bedroom and smother my screams into my pillow for hours at a time. I had frightening nightmares imagining how my sister died. I would bolt up in my bed shaking and trembling in fear wanting to run to my mom and dad for comfort because I was so very afraid. But, I never did that. Why? Because I listened to my mother crying herself to sleep night after night alone. My dad began staying away from the house into the wee hours of the night. I didn't know what was going on with them, so I kept my pain to myself.

Inside I felt like I was dying, but I didn't have a clue who I could tell. Really, I didn't even know if anyone would care what was happening with me. At age fifteen death isn't something you want to talk about with your friends, so my struggles escalated unnoticed by others.

I remember punishing myself. That was my way of working through some of the pain of my sister's death – certainly not a healthy way, I might add! My sister Carmella had been sick for seven years with asthma. Six months prior to her death she was ill with pneumonia. From the pneumonia she got other complications resulting in an enlarged and weakened heart. She struggled with eating and was very small and frail.

In my childish way of reasoning, I didn't think I deserved to be healthy so I ate very little for several months following her death. Every time food smelled good, I reminded myself I didn't deserve to eat. I felt weak and became very thin. It's interesting to me now as I think back that not one family member ever talked to me about my weight loss or the way I isolated myself from others. Talk about miscommunication! I took their inability to recognize any of my pain as meaning they didn't care. In fact, I remember screaming one day at my mother, asking her why she hated me so much. She just stared at me with a blank look. I honestly don't think she was able to see beyond her grief at that point in her life.

Blame and punishment often go hand-in-hand. I continued to blame and punish by not giving myself permission to have any fun. I turned sixteen the month my sister died, and I passed my driver's test soon after. The interesting thing is I wouldn't leave the house except for school. I isolated myself for months after my sister's death. Why? I didn't think I deserved to smile or to have fun. Instead, I lied to my friends when they invited me out. "My mom said I have to stay home. I don't know why, but she won't let me go out tonight."

I can still see my bedroom, and I still get anxious remembering what it felt like during those lonely, frightening months after my sister's death. I wrote her a lot of letters and hid them in a shoe box under my bed. In those letters I begged her to forgive me for not being a better sister. I felt so responsible for not taking better care of her when she was sick. Night after night, the hours of sobbing would continue.

I share this part of my life with you to give you some insight into a sibling's grief. I needed my mom and dad to talk to me. I needed somebody – anybody – to tell me it was okay for me to be alive. I needed someone to explain to me that nightmares are common following the death of a child. I needed someone to tell me what I was feeling was normal. I needed someone to give me permission to smile again.

Parents are consumed with their own grief, but their living children suffer grief, too. Childhood depression following sibling loss is very common and needs attention and intervention. Many siblings experience depression, anger, rage, self-inflicted pain, eating disorders, aggression, or withdrawn behavior, and suicidal thoughts. Their pain is real – just as real as the pain their parents are feeling. It's so important to validate and acknowledge the grief that siblings experience.

Families going through the grief of child loss are families in crisis. It is of utmost importance to pay attention to the siblings when a death has occurred. They have great need of support, but they don't know where to go to get that support. If you have a close friend or group of friends who will "adopt" your child for a while that would be so helpful and beneficial to the child. Children are just that – children. They crave the love of their parents, and for a while following the loss of a child parents are too consumed with their own grief to see clearly. Please, parents, if you are unable to give attention to your living children during this critical time, ask for help from other family members and friends. Ask if they will include your child in some normal family life. Ask them to invite your child to some picnics or the movies. Anything will do – just help them feel included, cared for, and loved.

Note: *If you notice extreme behavior such as cutting, severe depression and isolation, or any suicidal signs in your child, seek immediate medical help!*

What about grandparents? If your family is so fortunate to have grandparents who are involved members of your family, then child loss is going to greatly impact their lives, too. When a child dies a grandparent has a double blow to his or her heart. Grandparents grieve the loss of their grandchild, but they will also deeply mourn the loss because of seeing pain in their adult child's life. As parents, we hurt when our children hurt, and our natural response is to want to take away all of our child's pain immediately. We know that's an impossibility with child loss. The pain of grief is a journey and sadly there is no quick fix to ending the pain of child loss.

As with siblings, grandparents are often the overlooked and forgotten grievers. For some unknown reason we often put them on a pedestal and expect near perfection from grandparents. We expect them to be calm, remain strong during any situation, be available to help at all times, and to always know what to say and do during a crisis. What an insurmountable burden we mistakenly place on grandparents! It is only recently that grandparents have begun to share their thoughts and pain about child loss with others. Thankfully, grandparents can now get support through such agencies as The Compassionate Friends, GriefHaven.org, and SilentGriefSupport.com. What a blessing to finally validate and acknowledge how deeply grandparents grieve the loss of their grandchild.

Grandparents have a special bond with their grandchildren – a bond that is far, far different in many ways than they have with their own child. Part of the difference in the grandparent relationship is due to age and wisdom acquired with life experiences. And, part of this unique relationship grandparents have with their grandchildren is knowing that grandchildren will look to them for stability and strength that isn't often found in younger parents who are so involved and consumed with the everyday stresses of life.

As a child, I loved visiting my grandmother simply because she always had time for me. She never seemed rushed. Never do I remember her fussing with house cleaning or laundry when I visited her. She made certain that her focus was just on me, and I loved that!

Think about the void left in a grandparent's heart when a grandchild dies. There is such a loss and feeling of helplessness. Often grandparents will tell you they literally live for those moments when they can spend precious time with their grandchildren. To lose a grandchild is often losing a large part of a grandparent's joy and purpose for living.

In taking time to talk briefly about some of the different ways family members grieve the loss of a child, I hope you have a clearer view of how child loss impacts the dynamics of a family. Everyone in the family unit is grieving, and each is doing so in his or her own unique way. The family feels very broken for a long, long time following child loss. Losing a child is like being tossed to and fro in the middle of the sea during a raging storm without the captain of the ship. Everyone holds on for dear life and hopes to make it to shore.

Please save yourself and your family additional pain by communicating with each other. Ask how you can help. Ask what hurts the worst. Ask what you think you could do as a family to honor and remember the child that is now gone. Come up with a plan that is a "family plan" – a plan that will draw you together as a family unit.

Discuss such things as how you will get through all of the firsts – the first birthday, the first Thanksgiving, the first Christmas, and the first family vacation. Be sure to include siblings and grandparents in these planning sessions.

Will this be comfortable or easy to do? Absolutely not! This is a new journey for each one and this is totally uncharted territory. Do it anyway. You'll be so glad that you stepped out of your comfort zone and made very real efforts to draw closer as a family. Lines of communication will open, and your grief will not seem so raw when you are all talking and working together.

If you feel this is too difficult for you to do on your own, then seek the help of a trained professional to help open up avenues of communication. Your family has experienced the worst kind of trauma known to mankind – the death of a child. When you strive to find help, you will be surprised at how much stronger your family will become. You will learn to openly express your grief, and this is so vital in keeping the family healthy and strong.

Remember that you don't have to become a statistic! Even through the death of a child, you can still be a family and make precious memories together while including your child who has now gone on before you.

The key to keeping your family united is learning how to communicate effectively through grief!

7 WHAT'S THIS THING CALLED THE NEW NORMAL?

When child loss occurs, we take on a whole new language. We use words like rainbow baby, angelversary, members of the club, and the new normal. We talk as though we are familiar with these new words when in reality we're learning the true meaning of this new language little-by-little as we live in this foreign place called our new normal.

What exactly does it mean to now be living in the new normal? The short definition of life in the new normal is that as a bereaved parent we have now taken on a new appearance – not physically so much as emotionally. The longer definition is a bit more complicated and that's what we will talk about in this chapter. We will delve more deeply into what it means to be living in a place called the new normal.

It is an established fact that we are no longer the same person after child loss. We don't think the same way as we did before our child died. Our priorities in life have changed. We now see the world through different eyes. The innocence of life has been stripped away from us, and we now view life through eyes that have been stained with tears. Our emotions have changed dramatically. We are no longer naïve and innocent about what can happen in life. We see every situation as a potential for pain and loss. We are filled with fear.

The new normal is the place where we land after the reality of child loss settles in our hearts.

Habits, attitudes, and emotions all change following the loss of a child. Often, we will abandon our family traditions and find new ways of acknowledging birthdays, anniversaries, and special occasions within the family. This sudden dramatic shift from the norm is often confusing and upsetting to other members of the family because they want nothing more than to go back to how things were before child loss entered the picture. They want things to be "normal" – free of this thing we call grief. But, we know that life will never, ever be the same again – at least not for us. How could they be? We've just experienced the most earth-shattering, life changing trauma that can ever be experienced.

Our child is gone and so is that place called normal. Child loss is something that nobody can fix - ever! We gradually find a method to live life in a way that will be established as our "new normal" - different and apart from how we used to be.

When a child dies it feels as though our safety net has been cut from under us and we are free-falling into a cavern that is dark and frightening. We fight hard to figure out how to live in this place that is totally unfamiliar to us. Our traditions and values that we once held so dear to us no longer fit into our new normal. We are changed; therefore, change in every area of our lives is imminent.

We are by nature creatures of habit, so the changes that come about are not easy. We fight them with all of our being. We often don't like who we have become or the way we now wrestle with daily life. Even the little things in life turn into big things. Before our child's death there were four chairs occupied at the table. Now there are three chairs and the fourth is empty. Suddenly we don't know what to do. Where should the fourth chair go? What about the table? There used to be four plates sitting on the table and now there are three. Who sits where? It's too painful to see the empty place so we struggle to find a new normal – something that feels right. We try to find something that fits. Do you see how even the smallest change in daily living can send us into a tailspin of grief and wild emotions? Do you understand why we fight so hard to find our new normal in everyday life?

Child loss brings about so many unexpected changes. Every area of our life is affected. We now struggle with emotions such as anger and intense fear. Although we don't want to be angry, anger makes its way into our hearts and often becomes a part of our new normal. Anger can invade a normally quiet, agreeable person, turning him into a very vocal, disagreeable person. What is this anger all about? Anger is a normal grief response. Parents feel angry that their child had to be the one that died. It is normal for parents to feel angry when they see other parents with several children, and their only child has died. Parents may get very angry when family and friends don't acknowledge their child's death. Parents feel very angry to have been given such a load of unfair pain.

Parents don't like to fly off the handle at every little thing. It's no fun to feel mad at the world. But, the truth is that when a heart is hurting from the inside out, the pain wells up and becomes too much to bear and often shows itself as anger.

Often we get angry at the way our child died. Drunk drivers are responsible for thousands of deaths each year – all of them preventable if the person drinking would have stayed away from the wheel of a car. Cancer and heart disease take the lives of so many children – and often there are months of agony and suffering involved before the death of the child. Our pain turns into anger. We're angry because our child died senselessly. We're angry because our child suffered so much and there was nothing we could do to prevent the pain.

Addiction. Death by suicide. Murders. Drownings. We don't understand who we are any more without our child. All we know is that our heart is broken and there is nothing that can fix it. And, we're angry and afraid of this new normal that we are now living.

Every moment of every day there is an inner nagging fear that resides in parents of child loss. If this terrible thing can happen once, it can happen again. This thought is a distressing voice that replays in our minds over and over again. Before our child died, we never had thoughts like this. We barely grunted a good-bye when our child rushed out the door to football practice or to school. We expected our child to return. But, when the unimaginable happens, we change. Our thoughts change. Our hearts change. Anyone who lives with daily pain changes, and child loss is the worst pain that ever can be felt.

Our new normal is filled with so much fear. Fear breeds anxiety and anxiety can run out of control. We are never fully relaxed. We're always walking on the edge of panic. We don't know how to get this new self into a better place. In the initial months following child loss, we know we are changing. We know for certain we are not the same person we were before our child died. That is a hard fact to accept! And, it's very hard to like who we have become.

It feels as though we have another person living inside of us and we don't want that person there, but we have no idea how to make that person inside leave. Our new normal is far from glamorous!

Grief is not an easy walk and deserves lots of time and attention. If you try to stuff your grief down or shove it aside at this point in your grief journey, your new normal is going to be far more difficult and challenging than you ever thought.

Pain and grief deserve acknowledgement. It's impossible to repair what has happened. And, there is no fairy tale ending to this story of child loss. Our new normal is challenging and we will struggle with it for the remainder of our days on this earth.

There is something that we should address at this point that is critical to living in our new normal. We are not going to please everyone. In fact, we will probably not please very many. We will be questioned as to why we're so angry, sad, confused, emotional, or irrational. There will be people who will get in our faces and tell us that this is our opportunity to create a new beginning. They will paint a very rosy picture for us and tell us that all is going to be well when deep inside we feel as though we are dying.

We will struggle with life. There will be days when we really don't like ourselves and the person we have become in our new normal.

Please remember that this is a time of adjustment. Everything – and I do mean everything – in our life has changed. We are now feeling the pain of that huge hole left by the absence of our child more than ever before. And, we are feeling the pressure to accept life and move forward. We know that others around us need us, especially if there are still young children in our home. Intellectually we can reason it out that there is still beauty in this world, and life was meant to be lived. We understand that we can and must eventually find a place that feels okay – a place where we can call "home" within ourselves.

The struggle is real. The pain is real. The changes are real. Our new normal is developing and we know it. And, we are afraid. Afraid to let go. Afraid to trust. Afraid to smile. Afraid to relax. Afraid to stop crying. Why? Because fear is a safe hiding place. Fear has a way of masking some of the pain of grief.

Fear has a way of stopping us from walking into the reality of our new normal.

I will get a bit personal here and share with you a bit of my new normal in hopes that it will help you and give you some hope.

I have suffered six miscarriages, one of my sons was stillborn, and one of my adult sons died very unexpectedly at the age of forty-two from a massive heart attack. My heart has been shattered. Just about when I think I'm able to stand up and walk, another wave seems to come along and knock me back down.

Due to so much loss in my life, I am a changed person. But, not all of the changes have been negative. Because I grew up in an abusive household, neither of my parents ever said "I love you" to me. And, that made it extremely difficult for me to verbalize those words with others. Now that I know how fragile life is, I can say "I love you" and feel comfortable saying it frequently from deep within my heart, and that feels so good! Because I know the sorrow of saying good-bye without saying "I love you," my new normal says "I love you" often. I am so thankful for this part of my new normal!

I have become more aware of the pain others face due to my own pain. It's easy to get caught up in our own world and not see the challenges and pain of others. My eyes and ears have been changed due to child loss. My new normal now listens more attentively, and I see and feel so much more of the pain of others that I didn't identify with before my own losses. This is a difficult world in which we live. There is so much unfairness, so much sickness, and so much pain. There is so much child loss. Every child that dies is one too many. I now see more clearly in my new normal. I'm far more patient with others. Because I've had days when I've been short-tempered with others due to my inner pain, I now see people through different eyes. Maybe – just maybe – they are also agonizing over the pain of a loss. Maybe they are feeling similar pain to what I'm feeling. Maybe they need love, as I need love.

Every sunrise and sunset has special meaning to me. I usually use the evening sunset as my time to reflect on the day, and that's also when I do my crying. There's no doubt that my heart will forever feel broken. So much of the beauty of this life has been snatched away. But, with each new sunrise I force myself to say a word of thanks for something – even if it's for the pillow that cradles my throbbing head. I was so busy before my losses that I often went days, weeks, and sometimes months without saying thank you for the many, many good things in life I've been given. Food. Shelter. A job. Friends. A family. I have the basics in life which are really enough. Anything else is more than I could ever ask for or ever deserve.

My new normal is a time of inner reflection. I was building up a lot of anger and jealously, and I didn't like that part of myself. I felt as though life had been so unfair to me – and really there have been lots of unfair things that have happened to me. But, that's true for everyone. And, it has just been of late since the recent death of my adult son that I can see this and release the anger and jealousy that had been building up inside of me.

Yes, there's still plenty about my new normal that is hard – very, very hard. I don't think I'll ever be able to look at life the same way again. In fact, I know I won't. My heart hurts every single day, and the pain is throbbing, stabbing, and sometimes so bad that I feel like my heart is going to burst my chest wide open.

But, my new normal is teaching me that I'm not alone. Others suffer in this world, too, and when I really and truly think about that it helps me to not feel so alone. I don't feel so singled out anymore.

What I'm trying to say is this: Child loss changes all of us. It changes us in ways that we don't always like. But, some of the changes are ones that give us a new way to look at life. These changes allow us to take off our masks, be real, and share our lives in a way that we never did before.

In the early months of our grief walk, our new normal is frightening. We've been thrown into a place in life that we never asked for, and we're in a place where we don't want to be. But, we've also come to realize that there are others living this new normal, too, and that makes us a community. And, that makes us friends. And, that makes everything feel less scary.

Our new normal gives us a reason to love life and others with a passion that we've never felt before because we can now understand that we are not alone. Our pain is shared by many others. This new way of living and loving life will teach us how to gradually adjust to our new normal.

While in this adjustment period of our new normal, it helps to recognize the many changes that are taking place. It helps to embrace the good – the ways we now see life as more fragile and more precious than ever before. It helps to meet our pain head-on and accept ourselves for who we are in the present moment. We're not always who we want to be, but if we acknowledge that, we can learn to love our new selves and that's so important in finding a place where we can feel comfortable living in our new normal.

Don't try to fix your pain because it won't work. Instead, learn to see your pain for what it is, and by doing that you will eventually learn to re-enter life again and find your place of the new normal that is uniquely yours. Our child is not here with us on this earth, but we can reserve a special place for our child to be forever remembered in our home of the new normal.

8 IS THERE ANYTHING THAT WILL HELP?

The age-old question associated with the pain of child loss is, "Is there anything that will help?" We want to know what to do that will ease this burden of pain. We *need* to know what will help because we know that we can't go on like this forever. The pain is just too much!

Everybody seems to have a different answer to this, all alluding to the fact that there is nothing that will ever take away all of the pain of losing a child. While I know that to be true, there are some things we can do that will help ease this burden of pain.

Very soon after the loss of my baby boy Samuel I knew I needed to "do" something that would help make me feel better. That something for me was to begin a perennial flower garden. I can remember so well the first bag of daffodil bulbs I bought and planted in memory of Samuel. I chose the colors of the daffodils so carefully. His hair was fluffy and blond and reminded me of duck down. I knew I needed to choose a soft, pastel color and I was thrilled when I found just what I wanted. I planted fifty daffodil bulbs in memory of Samuel that fall. And, for every fall since (twenty-five now) I have added fifty new daffodil bulbs along with some other perennial flower bulbs. There is such a feeling of comfort and renewal when I wait for the first signs of these plants to push their way through the soil that was frozen from our harsh winters in the northeast. I now have literally thousands of blooms that decorate my landscape every spring in memory of my baby boy! For me, working outside in the soil, and creating a memorial garden for my baby boy is a visual that has helped me so much. And, many friends have been the happy recipients of gorgeous spring blooms.

Does a flower garden take away the pain of child loss? Absolutely not! Does it help? For me, there is joy found in the new life of a fresh spring flower garden bursting forth in full bloom every year. Many other parents have found flower gardens to help them, also.

We can do such things as keeping a journal, which is very therapeutic and helpful. By writing our thoughts, we release a bit of the pain. We also validate our child, and that is so very important. Plus, we can return to our journal and read our thoughts and see how much we've moved forward in this journey of grief. It's so important for us to actually see that we are taking steps forward. And, one of the biggest fears parents of child loss have is that of forgetting. We're so afraid that we'll forget what our child's smile looked like. We're afraid we won't remember what our child's hair smelled like. We are afraid that we'll forget all of the little habits that made our child unique. When we journal, there is the relief of forgetting because we've put down on paper from our memory the very things we've chosen to remember. What a wonderful blessing and help it is to have a journal of thoughts about our child!

We can choose to do things such as a balloon release on our child's birthday. We can bake a cake and invite friends who were close to our child and sit around a campfire and share wonderful stories about our child. Oh, how much that helps!

Many parents have chosen to begin a scholarship in memory of their child, and I think this is such a wonderful idea. We are creating something beautiful in memory of our child that gives to others in order to keep the memory of our child alive! The giving of the scholarship can be made into a special annual ceremony that gives you, the parent, the opportunity to share something special about your child and explain why you've created this scholarship in memory of your child. There is something very healing about knowing that your child's life is etched in history and will be remembered for years to come.

These are all things we've heard of parents doing in order to help lift the burden of pain of child loss. And, they do give inner satisfaction and peace knowing that we have created something beautiful as a way of remembering and honoring our child's life.

But, what about taking care of yourself following the loss of a child? Very seldom do we hear anything about the care of ourselves following the loss of a child, and I believe that self care is one of the most helpful things we can do.

You must take care of yourself following the loss of a child if you want to find your way back to living life again!

Think in very basic terms. When child loss occurs, we live in a fog for a while as described in Chapter 1. Then, we go through tremendous emotional turmoil including such things as lack of sleep, improper eating, and lack of exercise, panic attacks, extreme anxiety, fear, and mountains of stress. Our bodies and minds are out of kilter and we feel terrible. We may go to our doctor looking for help and he simply says that we need to learn how to relax more. Many times we're handed a pill and we're told that will help take away the pain.

Please know that I'm not against medication. In fact, following the death of my first son, I relied on medication to help me with high blood pressure that was stress induced, and I also needed something to help me fall asleep at night. Medication definitely helped me during the early months following the loss of my child. I think most of us are extremely thankful for the help medication can give us when taken properly.

In time, though, we need to think of other ways to get help with the basics of reentry into life. How does this happen? What helps us?

First we must take care of our physical selves. Make sure we're drinking enough water every day. Grief zaps our energy and depletes our bodies. Dehydration can occur very quickly when we're not drinking enough water. According to the Mayo Clinic, dehydration can occur rapidly and you cannot rely on feeling thirsty as being a sign of dehydration. Symptoms of dehydration may include headaches, dry skin, dizziness or lightheadedness, sunken eyes, rapid heartbeat, rapid breathing, and fever to name a few.[3] When we are grieving, we forget to do the basics such as drinking water and eating properly. We can help ourselves greatly by drinking plenty of fluids and making sure we get proper nutrition by eating three meals a day. Just by doing these two things, we are giving ourselves lots of help following the loss of a child. When we allow our bodies to get run down, we also are allowing our minds to get run down, and this grief cycle can become very hard to overcome and regain any kind of balance in health again.

If you've heard someone grieving the loss of their child say, "I'm so tired I feel like I can't move," it's probably safe to say that there is a bit of dehydration and improper nutrition to blame for feeling so physically immobilized!

What else helps us following the loss of a child? This sounds so basic, yet we often don't do this at all and we cause ourselves great harm. We must find a way of removing the grief mask and baring it all. What do I mean by that, and why is that so important?

When we mask our grief – cover it up – we are not facing it, and therefore we're repressing the pain. Eventually the pain of grief will work its way to the surface and that's often when a parent will feel like they are having an emotional breakdown. Life becomes too much to face, and all joy is gone. We are teetering on a balance beam, ready to fall off, and that's a very dangerous place to be.

When we face our grief head-on we will release a lot of the pain. Is this easy to do? Absolutely not! But, it's necessary to do! Nobody can do our grief work for us. This is one time that we must take some steps alone.

I know this sounds harsh to some, but in reality this is not at all harsh but the biggest gift we can possibly give to ourselves. After we've had the time to digest the reality of our loss, we must sit down face-to-face with our grief. This is frightening to do, and we can't do it all at once. It's like peeling an onion. We peel back the layers a little at a time.

The hardest, most difficult words we will ever say are, "My child died." But, until we can say those words and really grasp what they mean, we can never begin walking towards the light of hope. This is called facing our reality. When we can face the reality of our loss, we have taken a giant step forward in this journey of grief and it will feel like a 500-pound weight has been lifted off of our chest. Yes, we will cry. We will cry a million more tears. And, we might even feel worse for a while, but the truth is when we can say the words, "My child died," and have that face-to-face meeting with the reality of our loss we will begin to feel better.

The weight of wearing the grief mask has been lifted and we are now free to be ourselves!

I would be remiss if I didn't include prayer in this chapter about what helps. In the beginning of our grief walk following the loss of our child, we might be very angry with God, and on top of that we might be afraid to tell others about our anger with God. We don't want people to think badly of us, nor do we want to run the risk of thinking we will jeopardize our way into heaven. Our minds are working overtime when grieving the loss of our child, and it's common to think of things such as our faith, our spirituality, and of heaven. There comes a time when the majority of us will call out to God in our pain and anguish, and we rely heavily on prayer to help us.

According to WebMD, "For the past 30 years, Harvard scientist Herbert Benson, MD, has conducted his own studies on prayer. He focuses specifically on meditation, the Buddhist form of prayer, to understand how mind affects body. All forms of prayer, he says, evoke a relaxation response that quells stress, quiets the body, and promotes healing."[4] There have been numerous other studies done on the power of prayer, prayer and healing, and intercessory prayers, and all seem to have the same conclusion. Prayer works. They way prayer works for you is very individual, but the bottom line is if you are seeking help following the loss of a child, prayer will help you.

I'll interject a personal note here about prayer in my own life. Following the loss of my infant son, I was too upset with God to pray for a long, long time. But, I did ask others to pray for me. When someone looked me in the eyes and said they were praying specifically for me, I could feel an immediate response in my body. My shoulders began to relax, and my headache began to ease. Was it prayer or was it taking off my mask and becoming vulnerable enough to ask for prayer that helped? I believe it was both of those things.

Since the death of my adult son I have relied daily on prayer to help me. I often look to the heavens and feel the closeness of God and my son. There is a peace that overcomes me when I pray that gives me great relief. Even if you are not sure of your belief, I strongly recommend practicing prayer in order to get some help and relief from the pain of loss.

Just within the past ten years there has been a revival of the use of the yoga and meditation as a healing art. I'm so pleased to have Alex Howlett, a certified yoga instructor, share with us in the following section the way yoga and meditation can help when we are deeply grieving the loss of our child.

Using Yoga and Meditation to Heal Our Grief

As Clara already mentioned in Chapter 2, the sadness of losing your child will remain with you for a lifetime – a part of you is missing – but learning how to cope with the pain is not only possible, it's necessary. After experiencing a traumatic event, such as the death of a child, we convince ourselves that we can't go on with life. We become so consumed with what we can no longer have that our thoughts are either stuck in the past or in constant anxiety about the future.

Not only is the inability to stay grounded in the present moment bad for your spiritual and emotional health, but it also takes a major toll on your physical well-being. That is why the only thing left to do is learn to cope with the pain.

Doing so won't be easy. You'll probably feel like giving up, over and over. But you absolutely *must* make a commitment to consciously and continuously work on the things that will help you heal, for your own sake and for your loved ones. That may seem impossible at first, but taking small steps each day will help you in time to reach a point where your pain feels more manageable.

A traumatic experience in my life several years ago destroyed me, or so I thought. For the next three years, I suffered through chronic depression, panic attacks, nightmares, insomnia, intense anger, and flashbacks – all symptoms of post traumatic stress disorder. My emotions were constantly swinging between extreme sadness, rage, and total apathy towards life. Many times I wished that I would just fail to wake up one day so I could escape the pain. Over time, I began to recognize the things that allowed me to get through each day. So, I started to add in more of those things, until eventually I noticed that a lot of my trauma symptoms were either gone or much less frequent. Thinking back on my past, of course I still feel angry, hurt, and heartbroken. I still question why horrible things happen to good people. But the difference now is those thoughts and emotions don't control my life. Instead, I control my thoughts.

The most helpful tool in learning how to cope with my pain was yoga. In fact, practicing yoga was so helpful for my healing process I that became a certified instructor. I am now making it my life's purpose to teach people the same coping techniques that helped me find the strength to get to where I am today.

As you already know, everyone experiences the grief of child loss in a unique way, so everyone's healing journey will also be unique. A large factor in healing is finding your own coping methods, being patient (healing is not a fast or easy process by any means!) and being kind to yourself. I learned all of those things through my yoga practice, because of the many healing facets involved.

The union of mind, body, and spirit heals the whole person.

The word *yoga* means "union." The union that yoga practice creates is visible in a few different ways, one of which is the connection of the mind, body, and spirit. Your mind, body, and spirit work together in harmony, but when one or more of these components of your "whole self" is out of alignment, such as when you are grieving, your entire state of being suffers. When grief affects your emotional health through sadness, heartbreak, and emptiness, it also significantly affects your physical health. Grief manifests in the physical body, causing stress on the heart, increased blood pressure, difficulty sleeping, loss of appetite, a weakened immune system, tense muscles or muscle pain, and headaches. When anxiety is present along with your grief, you might experience shortness of breath, heart palpitations, chest pain, fatigue, and feeling faint.

Yoga teaches you how to realign the physical, mental, and emotional/spiritual bodies to allow holistic healing to take place. The practice of yoga does not encourage you to shut out your emotions, but rather to accept them and learn to live with them in a way that is no longer destructive to your health. Hatha yoga, the type of yoga that we practice in the western world, encourages the mind-body-spirit alignment through a combination of breathwork, physical postures, and meditation. Each of these components has a very specific purpose in bettering students' health.

Slow, mindful breaths help to calm your mind and body.

Breathwork, known in yoga as *pranayama*, or extension of the life force, calms your mind and centers your attention. It also stabilizes blood pressure and energy levels, reduces anxiety and stress, and relaxes the muscles. Our central nervous system is made up of two parts: sympathetic and parasympathetic. These two parts need to maintain proper balance to keep us healthy, but when we're grieving these systems are imbalanced. When you have anxious or racing thoughts for an extended period of time, the sympathetic nervous system is overworked. The paraysmpathetic nervous system, which is responsible for rest and digestion, needs to be activated to bring you back to a state of balance. Consciously taking steady, deep breaths stimulates the parasympathetic nervous system. This helps to slow down your heart rate, lower your blood pressure, and create a sense of calmness. Deep breathing also helps to reduce strain on your chest and neck, allowing those areas of your body to relax.

In addition to calming physical stress responses in the body, practicing deep, mindful breathing helps slow your mind's racing thoughts and any intense emotional energy you're experiencing. Particularly during yoga classes, teachers instruct students to focus their full attention on breathing, noticing the sensations of the air entering and leaving the body, and paying attention to the body's responses, such as the chest rising and falling and the belly expanding and contracting. This one-track thought process draws students' focus away from worries and fears and stimulates a relaxation response.

Try the following breathing exercise and take note of how your mind and body feel before and after:

Find a comfortable seated position. Inhale in through your nose, taking the air all the way down into your pelvic area. Notice your belly drop down and expand as your lungs fill with air. Now exhale out through your nose, and feel your belly contract in and up as you expel the air from your lungs. Keep your breathing even, making each inhalation and each exhalation take up the same amount of time. If it helps you to relax, close your eyes while continuing to take several more slow, deep breaths.

Start this exercise with ten slow, deep breaths, noting the changes you feel afterwards both physically and mentally. Do you feel more physically relaxed? Does your mind feel calmer? If this is a comfortable practice for you, increase the number of breaths daily, until you are able to sit and focus on breathing mindfully for ten minutes at a time. As you continue to practice this exercise, also see if you can slow down your breathing even more, maybe taking a full count to five for each inhalation and a count to five for each exhalation. As you practice this breathing exercise, try to keep your mind focused only on what you are doing: breathing, and letting all other thoughts float away.

If your mind starts to wander, it might be helpful for you to count your breaths as so, "Inhale, one. Exhale, one. Inhale, two. Exhale, two," until you reach a certain goal, and then count all the way back down to one. Another option to keep your mind centered is to repeat a positive mantra to yourself during this exercise, such as "I am relaxed," or "I am safe in the present moment." Over time, this will become easier and feel natural.

Releasing tension in our bodies also help us release stored up emotions.

There are several different ways the physical yoga postures, known as *asanas*, help us to cope with grief. As you likely already know, exercise releases endorphins, the "feel good hormones." Practicing yoga also regulates levels of cortisol, the hormone released in response to stress, which is dangerous when levels are too high or too low. The regulation of cortisol helps reduce stress, depression, and high blood pressure.

The physical postures of yoga also create balance by tapping into the mind-body connection. As noted before, symptoms of grief manifest in your physical body. Performing a sequence of yoga postures specifically designed to target affected areas of your body can release stored up emotions associated with that part of the body. It's common for people who are dealing with trauma or grief to experience an emotional breakthrough while practicing yoga. Your first time practicing yoga, you may suddenly find yourself in tears during a certain posture because of the release of stored up emotions. That sudden release of emotions or feeling of vulnerability may seem scary or uncomfortable at first, especially if you're not expecting it. However, know that you are okay. You are safe. Your first response may be to shut down and try to escape the pain, but if you expect this experience and welcome it, it can be a very helpful part of the healing process.

Meditation allows you to get to know your true self and become comfortable within your own body.

The grief of loss can cause your mind to get stuck in a loop, or repetitive pattern, of negative thoughts or negative self talk. You might keep reliving the tragic memory of finding out about the death of your child. Or perhaps your mind is overcome with a pattern of guilty thoughts, and you start to convince yourself that there are things you could have done or should have done to protect your child. These loops of self-criticism or racing thoughts are dangerous, because they pile up negative energy on top of negative energy until you feel completely defeated. This prolongs the healing process, and the dangerous cycle repeats itself until you learn how to break it. Your thoughts are very powerful, and they largely impact the way you experience the world. Challenging and changing these negative thought patterns is absolutely necessary to regain control in your life.

The meditative aspect of yoga can be a very effective tool for self-reflection and changing thought patterns. The first step towards reducing your negative thoughts is to be aware of them. Please remember that the sadness and pain of child loss are normal, healthy emotions that you should acknowledge and give yourself permission to feel. These are not at all part of the negative thoughts that we're working to change. The thoughts we are trying to challenge are the ones that are untrue – the ones that tell you that you can never feel happy again, that you should feel guilty, that you must have done something to deserve this loss, or that nobody cares about you. None of these things are true, and you need to remember that.

In yoga, there is a lot of emphasis on mindfulness, or surrendering to the present moment. During the breathing portion of class, or in the last few minutes of class, you may be led through a period of self-reflection or meditation. During this time, the purpose is to allow your emotions to arise naturally as your body is in a relaxed state. Give yourself permission to sit with these emotions, and as they pass, let them go. This period of self-reflection might bring up emotions of love, loss, emptiness, or sadness. If any harmful thoughts arise while you are in this guided state of meditation, like the ones we outlined above, now is the time to remind yourself again that they are untrue and release them from your mind. Letting go of harmful thought patterns will likely be really difficult and uncomfortable at first, but combining this mindfulness practice with deep, relaxed breathing makes it more effective, and it will become much easier over time. Meditation will allow you to invite in feelings of self-compassion and release feelings of guilt and shame.

Again, all of this will be challenging. Yoga is not a magical practice that will change your life after one class. It's an arduous journey of self-transformation that will take much time and much effort, but the effort you put in will be worth the healing results you will see. The more you practice, the more control you'll have over your mind. So, instead of feeling stuck with self-defeating thoughts, you'll learn how to let them go so you can be at peace with yourself.

Yoga helps us find a community of like-minded people.

While there are times you'll need to be alone during your grief journey, connecting with other people creates a sense of love, support, and encouragement. In Chapter 2, Clara noted several online communities where you can connect with others to share your journey of child loss and seek support in your darkest moments. In addition to support communities for child loss, you can find a sense of community through your yoga practice. Whether you decide to take live classes or start a home practice with online classes, you can connect with others who practice yoga as a form of healing.

The yoga community is full of people who have found refuge from pain through their yoga practice. They have gained the wisdom to accept life as it is and stop reliving painful memories. Try seeking out a trauma-informed yoga instructor or a yoga therapist near you to get help that is specific to grief. If you cannot find a certified trauma-informed or therapeutic yoga instructor in your area, any gentle yoga class will help you relax to work through your moments of intense grief.

Additional resources

Please feel free to contact me with any questions about yoga or meditation for grief. You may fill out a contact form or find out more on my website, AlexHowlettYoga.com, or email me directly at alexhowlettyoga@gmail.com. Please visit the following link to view and practice the Yoga for Grief video I have created for you: AlexHowlettYoga.com/yoga-for-grief.

~~~

As you can see, the information Alex gave us is vital to our well-being following the loss of our child. Rather than feeling totally lost and helpless, we now have tools that can be used every day to help us breathe better, sleep more easily, and relax. We know we must monitor our water and food intake to help keep our bodies and minds functioning well. There are activities that we can do that can help us to validate the life of our child and keep our child's memory alive. We know that prayer helps. We also have been given the many benefits of using different forms of meditation and the useful practice of yoga.

Most of all, please remember that when we take some form of action as mentioned in this chapter we are taking steps to empower and free ourselves from the bondage of grief! We are now taking steps to prepare us to enter life again!

9 WORKING HARD TO FIND HOPE

When a child dies so does our hope. We are a changed person in so many ways as we've already established in Chapter 7. Sadly, along with the many changes that take place with a broken heart, there is also a change that happens that we don't like to talk about. We lose hope. I would dare say that most parents who lose a child go through a period when all of life looks bleak, and they cannot think of a reason why they are still living. They would gladly have exchanged their life for their child's life. Search as they may, they cannot find a reason to be excited about life any more. Hope as they once knew it is gone.

Child loss gives such a blow to the heart that we see life through tear stained eyes. No longer does the sky look blue. Instead, we see ominous shadows looming overhead that seem to send us a message of doom. We drop to a low point in life when we want to give up. It feels like all is lost. There are no more dreams. No more expectations. No more fantasies about how wonderful life is going to be. No more goals to set – not without our child. Lost hope is now a part of every fiber within us, and it seems like an impossibility that life will ever be hopeful again.

When talking about hope in this chapter we are referencing not so much spiritual hope – the hope of heaven – but rather that expectation that something good will happen in our life here on earth. Hope is holding fast to anticipation that there are better days ahead. Hope is holding on when all logic tells us to let go. Hope is living rather than existing. Hope includes a feeling of trust. Since child loss happened, we no longer trust in life anymore. How can we when something as devastating as the loss of our child has happened? We feel fiercely betrayed and suddenly none of life makes sense anymore.

When our child died we became broken, but it's not the kind of broken that can be fixed. When a leg is broken, it is placed in a cast for a few weeks, and we know that when the cast is removed the leg will work properly again. We are certain that the broken bone will fuse together and heal. The pain will be gone, and the leg will continue on doing what is was designed to do. We anticipate the healing of that bone and plan on walking, running, jumping, and playing basketball again. Our days of recovery are filled with excitement and anticipation as we plan for fun times in the future following recovery. That's hope!

The picture is far different with a broken heart. There is nothing a doctor can do to heal the brokenness from child loss. Sure, there are medications that can help dull the pain for a while. But, there is nothing that will repair a heart that has been broken by the loss of a child. We know this because we are living with the brokenness. We know how deep the pain is and we have searched for answers – searched for ways to heal this brokenness – only to come back to our original thought that there is no hope of that happening.

So, what does a parent of child loss do? Do we live in a constant state of hopeless agony and pain for the remainder of our days on this earth? Sadly, many parents do get lost at this point in life. They let go too soon and allow hope to slowly drift away.

We struggle with the fact that we had no choice whatsoever about child loss. If we did, we never would have allowed our child to die. We were stripped of the miracle of our child and were left sitting in the ashes of brokenness searching for something to give us hope. But, we find none. At least we feel as though all hope vanished when our child left us.

As hard as this might sound, the truth is that bringing hope back into our lives becomes a choice that we must make. Many parents will turn away from this thought saying we are denied hope because our child is no longer here. Every reason for living has been taken away. Many have erringly convinced themselves that they do not deserve to feel the blessing of hope again so they give up on life.

There is however, a critical moment in our grief walk where we will be faced with making a decision. Will I choose hope or will I choose to remain wrapped in a blanket of smothering pain for the rest of my life? That's tough to hear! It's even more difficult to believe. Even worse, we have to convince ourselves that eventually we will feel a glimmer of hope within us.

When we think of hope as a choice, it becomes something that feels tangible and achievable. Hope becomes a goal to work towards. Hope is a challenge to accept the reality of our loss and to hold fast to the belief that life will again be worth living.

Is hope an easy choice? Absolutely not! Let me clear up a myth at this point. To believe that the pain and heartbreak of child loss will leave if we choose hope is a misconception. If someone tells you that you will find true healing from child loss, they have never walked this lonely, broken journey that you are traveling. If you have people telling you that you're weak in faith because you are feeling broken and hopeless they've never been to this point in their own life. Your faith is not measured by your grief. You will grieve the loss of your child until the day you leave this earth, but you can regain hope in your life. And, that is a beautiful thought!

How do we do this? How do we find hope after losing a child? How do we choose hope over despair? *We do this by first making a very conscious decision that we will eventually live a life of hope.* We make this decision by taking baby steps – little-by-little we begin telling ourselves that we can do this. We can and we must choose hope if we want to push ourselves out of the embalming force of constant pain. Do you remember in the very first chapter of this book when we talked about the fact that everyone wants to avoid pain at all cost? We have come full circle and now we are being faced to make that choice. If we choose hope all of our pain will not leave, but we will have a reason to live. To me, that sounds like a way of lightening the burden of pain that we've been buried under since the loss of our precious child.

I have an exercise for you to do. It's a very simple way of retraining our brains to think hopeful thoughts. Take a note card or Post-it note and write the word HOPE on it. Place this card where you can see it the first thing in the morning when you wake up and the last thing in the evening before you fall asleep. Look at the word. Say it aloud. Allow it to be your meditative word. HOPE. When your thoughts are full of despair and are swirling through your mind adding additional pain to your broken heart, pause and think of the word HOPE. Repeat the word HOPE over and over again until you begin to feel a bit of inner calm. This is how meditation works that was described in Chapter 8.

As a parents of child loss, you are searching so hard to find a reason to get up in the morning following the loss of your child, and that is not easy to do. So much of your future was lost when your child died that it's difficult to see beyond the pain of today. But, you are courageous. You are very courageous because you are here. Even living one day without your child takes great courage.

Finding a place and purpose in life is a huge undertaking. Our friends and family members want to fix us and they want to shove us out of our grief because they believe that will help us to find hope. Rather than help us, these well-meaning people often push us further down the tunnel of despair and we drift further away from finding hope.

So, let's get to the point and talk about what practical things you can do to help bring hope back into your life.

Think for a moment about what special qualities children have that we would like to incorporate into our own lives. Children are filled with curiosity for all of life and they are energized by hope. Maybe, just maybe, we need to become more like children in our thinking if we want to bring hope back into our lives. Do you remember the joy of chasing after butterflies when you were a child? Do you remember the sheer excitement of splashing barefoot in mud puddles? Do you remember standing outside in the snow and licking snowflakes as they slowly fell from the sky? Do you remember taking off your shoes and wiggling your toes through the soft blades of springtime grass? Do you remember taking long walks and strolling along picking up shiny pebbles and sticks along the way? Do you remember lying down on a blanket under the stars and sucking in your breath as you blinked your eyes in amazement at the millions of twinkling stars shining in the sky? This is hope. This is what you're trying so hard to put back into your life. And, you can do it! No, it will not be the same experience as when you had your child with you, but you can learn to be excited and hopeful about life once again.

By thinking hope-filled thoughts you will slowly begin to see life through eyes of hope!

What else helps? *Give yourself permission to live in your pain.* The harder you fight against the pain, the more tense you will become, the more depressed you will be, and the darker your thoughts will become. By allowing yourself to feel your pain you will face it and find out that you are much, much stronger than you thought. Fear immobilizes us. Fear crushes our spirit. Fear can overcome us. But, hope is stronger than fear. Stop being afraid of your pain and allow yourself to feel it. I know that probably sounds foreign to what we've always been taught. We're taught that if we have a headache we immediately reach for two Tylenol tablets to make the headache go away. What if we worked through the headache? What if we allowed ourselves to feel the headache – or the pain – and stopped resisting it? Do you know that tension and fear increase our pain? According to a study published in the journal *Pain*, Sean Mackey, MD, PhD, and co-author of the study says, "If we can learn to control the fear about pain maybe that will help us better control the pain."[5]

When we stop fighting and fearing the pain of child loss, we will be more able to control the pain and allow room for hope to enter our lives again! I don't know about you, but I find a great deal of comfort and hope in knowing that I will benefit from facing my pain. It's exhausting running from pain. It's draining trying to hide our pain. It's frightening to always shove our pain aside because we never know when it's going to resurface again with a vengeance.

We also need to learn how to pause in this thing called child loss. What do I mean by that? When child loss took place, there were a thousand and one different changes taking place at the same time in our life. Our emotions were in turmoil. Grief was exhausting and caused our bodies and minds to feel overly tired, drained, and depleted. There were family conflicts and misunderstandings. Nothing felt normal or right in our lives anymore and our minds were running at such a fast pace that it was impossible to keep up with all of the changes.

Pause. Stop. Breathe.

When we give ourselves the gift of pausing – taking a time out – we are giving ourselves the opportunity to rest our sorrowful, hopeless thoughts and we are making room for hope to enter our minds. Isn't that a wonderful thought? Just repeating the words gives us hope. Pause. Stop. Breathe.

Stop trying to fix yourself! Stay present to whatever has erupted in your life and feel it, face it, then pause and breathe. But, please don't be judgmental of yourself and expect perfection because it's not going to happen. You have just experienced the worst heartbreak that anyone can ever experience. The fact that your child died is not going to go away. The fact that your heart has been broken is not going to change.

Stop trying to fix what cannot be fixed. Rather learn to live your life in this brokenness and begin to rewrite your story.

By loving yourself. By forgiving yourself. By realizing that your life is what it is – a life without your child – you will begin to feel a shift in your thinking. By understanding that there is nothing that will ever be fair trade for your child's life, you will begin to accept the life you now have. You will begin to feel a new kind of energy stir within your soul. You will begin to feel an ever so small flicker of hope. And, that flicker of hope is your life-sustaining gift.

Let me stop here for just a moment and say that I am not at all minimizing the pain of losing a child. That pain will always and forever be part of the new you. We discussed that in full detail in Chapter 7. But, what you can do is finally come to an acceptance of what has happened. Does that mean you'll feel good about losing your child? Never! Does that mean that you'll see a silver lining following child loss? I don't think so. In fact I know that there is no silver lining – no happy blessing that comes from losing a child. Does this mean that you'll have a storybook ending with roses and smiles and fairies dancing all around? Absolutely not! What it means is you now are given a choice – *the choice to begin rewriting your story* – by including your pain and including your child and including hope!

I found it extremely difficult to find hope following loss in my own life. When I delivered my stillborn baby boy Samuel, as I mentioned in a previous chapter, there were moments when I felt like giving up. I even felt moments of such despair that I felt like dying. I saw no reason to live. But, hope has a way of slipping into the cracks of our broken hearts in ways that we least expect.

I can remember the exact moment when I began to rewrite the story of my life in my brokenness. It was a hot August afternoon and I was outside. I had been crying, and I didn't want my other children to see me crying again. It's scary for young children to see their mom unable to do much except shed tears. I kept thinking, "I can't do this anymore. I just can't. I don't want to do this anymore. It's too hard." I sucked in my breath in order to stifle my sobs that were ready to erupt when a butterfly came by and sat on my left arm. I tried to swoosh it away, but the butterfly wouldn't move. I kept looking at its wings and how beautiful they were. And, that butterfly seemed to be looking at me. It fluttered, then lit on the side of my face as if to dry my tears. It was at that moment that I saw beauty for the first time since Samuel's death. I remember touching my cheek where the butterfly was and thinking, "God sent this for me. This is my gift."

To some people a butterfly is just another insect, but to me the symbolism of hope at that moment of my deepest despair will stay will me forever. Years before the death of my baby boy a friend had given me a book, *Hope for the Flowers* by Trina Paulus. On the cover of the book is a quote I memorized. "How does one become a butterfly? You must want to fly so much that you are willing to give up being a caterpillar."

In my darkest moment, hope came to me in the form of a butterfly and I knew – I absolutely knew – that was my defining moment. That was the moment I made the choice to give up being a caterpillar and I began to rewrite the story of my life.

Practice fiercely loving others in a world that is unfair, in a world where children die, in a world where there are horrible diseases, and in a world where terrible things happen to beautiful people. Love is the connector to hope.

When we love within our life of pain, we love with completeness. We love with honesty. We love with acceptance of others. We love with forgiveness. We love with passion. We love with courage. We love with bravery. We love with an expectation and a desire to help others in their brokenness. We love with trust.

And, this wildly passionate love for others and ourselves is what rebuilds the story of our broken lives with hope.

10 REST IN HEAVEN, MY DEAR CHILD

At the end of the day when the sun goes down and we are all alone with our thoughts we strip away the veneer of child loss and bare our souls. How lonely and frightening those moments of being alone with our thoughts can be! We think of everything meaningful to us, and of course at the top of our thoughts is our child – our precious child – who has left this earth far too soon.

As a mother of child loss I often find it difficult to sleep at night. I live alone and keep extremely busy during the day, but nighttime is different. It is just me and my thoughts. I have made it a habit to think about my blessings, and I have many blessings as we all do. Inevitably my thoughts turn to my children. I think about where they are in their lives. Are they happy? Are they fulfilled with the work they are doing? Of course I do my fair share of worrying as most parents do. Then, my thoughts shift from my children here on earth to my children who have died. Death seems like such a cruel word to say – especially at night when we are surrounded only by darkness.

I wonder about heaven. I wonder if heaven is real. I, like you, have wished so much that I could have one of those

91

experiences that we read about where people are pronounced dead and then come back to tell of their near-death experience. I've read so many of those stories where people have experienced the feeling of going through a tunnel and seeing a bright light shining – so bright that it is warm and only emits love. Others have said they have gone to a place that is so beautiful and there is a struggle between life and death – between heaven and earth. They have no fear any more of dying. Oh, how we, as parents of child loss wish we could experience that so that we'd know for sure where our child is now that he is gone.

Those of us who profess to believe in God and an afterlife say we believe in heaven. That being said, I must confess that since I have experienced child loss I want to know more about this place called heaven. Every parent wants to know more because we want to be *absolutely certain* that our child is safe from all harm. We need to know that our child is not in pain. We beg God through our daily prayers to allow us to know more of this place called heaven.

We form very clear mental pictures as to what heaven is like, and our minds grow peaceful as we envision our child surrounded by pure, holy love. It is a great comfort to believe that our child is now in a place where all struggles are gone. Our child is now safe in a place where there is no more sickness, there is no fear, and there are no more tears. Can you truly imagine your child living in a perfect place like that? When our anxious thoughts begin running wild, thoughts of heaven calm us down. Heaven is our eternal lifeline that we cling to every hour of the day.

Many of us have had the treasured experience of receiving signs from our child reassuring us that our child is safe and well. These signs might come in the form of a dream. We also might experience a very literal sign – something that cannot be explained according to human terms. I remember one such experience following the death of my infant son Samuel. Years before Samuel was delivered stillborn, I bought a small cactus plant that was in full bloom. The flower was bright red and expanded across the entire width of the plant. Within months of purchasing that plant, the flower dried up and fell off. This particular cactus was supposed to bloom two times a year, but it never did. I tried everything to encourage that plant to blossom. I fed it fertilizer. I gave it the correct light it needed. I even transplanted it with a specialized cactus soil that guaranteed blooms. Still nothing happened.

This went on for seven years until one day – *during the first autumn following the loss of my baby Samuel* – I realized that this plant was never going to produce a flower. It was nothing but a short, stubbly plant with a lot of prickly thorns. Definitely not pretty! So, I tossed it outside on my burn pile. I still remember the day because I was feeling so distraught, so discouraged, and so hopeless following the loss of my baby. This cactus seemed like one more reminder of abandoned hope. I admit that when I threw this plant onto the burn pile I did so with anger. I didn't need one more reminder of something that was void of life!

When spring arrived and the snow melted, I tossed some final trash onto the pile to be burned. Out of the corner of my eye I spotted something colorful peeking out from beneath the burn pile. I moved some wood aside to see what was there, and I stood with my mouth wide open in shock and in total amazement. Beneath that pile of debris was the sign that I had been praying for with every breath in me. There – right before my eyes – was that tiny cactus plant *in full bloom*!

How was this possible? That particular winter had been harsh – brutally cold with lots of snow. Yet here, in my hands, was living proof of a miracle. This was the first spring without baby Samuel, and in my hands I was holding a

93

perfect blossom from what should have been a dead plant. That was my sign that there is life beyond the grave. That was my sign – the sign I needed to prove to me that heaven is real. That was my sign of hope.

I'm not a person who readily believes stories like this. In fact, it's my nature to question so-called miracles. But, I can't deny what I saw. I took pictures of that blooming cactus to serve as a reminder to me that there is some kind of life beyond the grave. When I begin to question, I look at that picture and I am refueled with much-needed hope. Child loss leaves us so empty and so full of questions without any answers!

Many have lost children to horrific accidents and sorrowful circumstances such as cancer, murders, or suicide. There is never a good way that a child dies. There is so much pain when our thoughts are focused on how our child died. Believe me when I say I personally know how our thoughts can travel very quickly to the traumatic thoughts of how our child died. But, when we have an experience such as I did with the blooming cactus, we can change our focus to the belief of heaven and the joy of knowing that our child's life will bloom forever!

What if you haven't had such an experience yet? I can't promise that you will ever have that defining moment when you know with absolute certainty that there is an afterlife and a place where your child resides called heaven. But, I can assure you that we have been given descriptions of heaven by many others and we can choose to believe. We can choose to trust. We can choose to have faith and hold fast to that belief, and when we do our hearts are calmed and our fears begin to dissolve.

I would be remiss if I didn't quote some from the most famous book of all time – the Bible. Researcher James

Chapman has compiled a list of the most read books in the world. Chapman created the list by examining how many individual copies of the books had been printed and sold over the last 50 years. According to the list, the Bible leads the countdown by a large margin, with nearly 4 billion copies printed and sold globally in the last five decades. *Quotations from the Works of Mao Tse-tung* was number two (820 million copies), followed by the *Harry Potter* series (400 million copies), *The Lord of the Rings* trilogy (103 million), and Paulo Coelho's *The Alchemist* (65 million). [6]

According to the Bible, **heaven is God's dwelling place**. Just a few Scriptures you can look up on your own are: Deuteronomy 26:15, Psalm 2:4, Psalm 23:1, Isaiah 57:15, Matthew 10:32-33, and Revelation 21:22-27.

Add to that, the fact that **heaven, according to the Bible, will be beautiful**. (Revelation 21:2, 11, 18, 19, 21)

There's more to help us in our quest to believe in heaven! In describing heaven, the Bible tells us much about what will *not* be there.

There will be no sickness in heaven. (Revelation 21:4)

There will be no sorrow, or crying, or mourning in heaven. (Revelation 7:17, Revelation 21:4)

There will be no hunger or thirst in heaven. (Revelation 7:16-17)

There will be no more death in heaven. (Luke 20:36, Revelation 21:4)

Heaven is a place of rest. (2 Thessalonians 1:7, Hebrews 4:9, Revelation 14:3)

Heaven is described in Scriptures, perhaps figuratively, as "up" in the sky. (2 Kings 2:11, Acts 7:55-56)

I know that our faith gets uprooted during the deep, raw moments of child loss. We question everything about our faith, including our belief in heaven. But, most times we come full-circle back to our core belief that there is a resting place – a place prepared for us and our child. There is a place where there is only love and peace and beauty. A place where only joy resides. And, that place is called heaven.

There are many who do not believe in an afterlife of any kind, and hearing things like there is a heaven provides no comfort at all. But, we can still have hope – the hope that our child is at rest. We can hold fast to the thought that our child is at peace. This is especially comforting to think of when a child suffered from an illness and lived with endless pain. Now, we can say, "Rest, my precious child. Rest."

I especially would like to address the subject of suicide before closing this chapter. One day I hope to devote an entire book to the loss of a child by suicide, because I think it is one of the most misunderstood losses of all and leaves parents with such a burden of guilt coupled with so many questions that will never be answered. Whether or not you believe in heaven or any kind of afterlife, I do hope that you can receive a measure of internal peace knowing that your child is finally at rest. Any type of mental illness leading to suicide, ranging from depression to bipolar disorder, to schizophrenia, to post traumatic illnesses are by and large misunderstood by most of us. There is also such a stigma attached to mental illness that we are often fearful to say that our child struggled with depression or was diagnosed with a mental illness. Oh, how I long for the day when that stigma is banished! This misinformation has caused so much needless pain to everyone involved.

If your child died from suicide, please stop blaming yourself. There is nobody to blame. We don't yet understand what goes on inside the mind to bring a person to the point of ending his or her own life. We do know that it is not your fault. According to the Hopeline,[7] "people who commit suicide feel hopeless. They are hurting so badly they want the pain to end." What causes such extreme hopelessness? We don't have the answer to that yet, but one thing is for certain. It is nothing that you did or did not do that caused your child to feel this way.

No matter what your belief about heaven, an afterlife, or no afterlife, please allow yourself to be comforted by understanding that your child is no longer living in a daily state of hopelessness. I know that this thought in no way makes up for the void left by your child, but hopefully your burden of guilt will be lifted and you can think of your child as being finally free from all pain – both mental and physical.

There is no such thing as "the end" of our grief journey. We are rewriting the story of our lives every day that we live without our child. It's not an easy story to write, but we can write this new story with love and with hope. How do we "live in our pain"? We do that by being brave. By being brave enough to tell the story of our child, including our child's death. The intense love we feel for our child includes our child's death. There are some things in this life that are never going to have a happy ending, and child loss is one of them. I'm not going to tell you that if you have thoughts of heaven, if you believe in some kind of afterlife, or if you believe that death is the final door through which we must pass, your pain of child loss will end.

The truth is that there are some things that just cannot be fixed, and child loss is one of them. There will forever be pain, so we must learn to be brave enough to acknowledge our pain. Tell your stories of love. Tell and retell the stories of your child's life – and your child's death. The birth and death of your child are so important to the new life story you are writing. Talk about the pause in-between. Talk about those moments that were funny. Keep those stories alive. And, talk about those stories that weren't so funny because those stories are as much a part of the love you had for your child as the happy ones.

Don't be afraid to create beautiful holiday traditions that are new, but also include the precious memory of your child. Do those things that feel right and good for you. Throw away the boundaries that others have set for you, and live your moments of grief in love. Love will guide you to know how to live in your pain. By practicing love in all that you do and in all that you think, you will learn to live in this imperfect world – a world where children die and suffering exists. Listen to your pain and be willing to write this new story. Write your story from love, because love is the only thing that lasts.

I'd like to close this chapter by saying that as parents we will forever miss our child while we remain in our temporary dwelling place here on earth. There is no magic formula that can ever take away that pain. No amount of faith will fix the grief of child loss. We will never heal from child loss – not in the sense that we will be whole again. There will always be a part of our heart that is missing. That part of us left the moment our child left this earth. But, we can experience genuine hope as we discussed in the previous chapter. We can experience hope within our pain. That takes great courage, and every parent, grandparent, and sibling of child loss is a person of courage.

We can also trust. We can trust in the hope that our child is at rest. It is that trust and that belief that will bring us what our weary souls need – peace.

There are a few sayings that have helped me during my most difficult moments of grief, and it is my hope and prayer that these closing remarks will help you, too.

"The mention of my child's name may bring tears to my eyes, but it never fails to bring music to my ears. Please let me hear the beautiful music of my child's name. It soothes my broken heart and sings to my soul."
~Unknown

Another thought that has helped me tremendously and I pray will help you, too:

"We can shed tears that he is gone. Or we can smile because he has lived. We can close our eyes and pray that he'll come back. Or we can open our eyes and see all that he has left for us to embrace. We can turn our back on tomorrow and live only in yesterday. Or, we can be happy tomorrow because of yesterday. We can remember only that he is gone. Or we can cherish his memory and continue to live on. We can cry and close our mind, be empty and turn our back. Or, we can do what he would want. We can smile, open our eyes, love, and go on. My child, my precious child, is gone but will never be forgotten." *~David Harkins*

A short poem that helps me when I am feeling so alone in my grief:

My Precious Child
You are near
Even if I don't see you.
You are with me
Even if you are far, far away.
You are in my every thought,
In every beat of my heart.
You fill my life
Always

~Unknown

And, so I close with this daily prayer of the heartbreak and hope of every parent of child loss:

Because of you I am able to say that I have experienced a love of the highest degree. My love for you cannot be expressed by mere words. My love for you is fierce and strong and can never be erased. The time I had with you was not nearly enough. Could time with my child ever be enough? There is one thing I want you to know. Your life was a miracle – my miracle – and will always be my greatest treasure. There is nothing that can ever separate us – not even this thing called death. Our hearts continue to beat as one, because the only thing I know for certain is love is the only thing that lasts. I love you with all of my being, and I always will. Without you my tomorrow wouldn't be worth the wait, and my yesterdays wouldn't be worth remembering. Rest, my child. Rest in heaven, my precious, precious child.

ENDNOTES

[1] See Chapter 8 for a more detailed explanation of how yoga and meditation work to help relieve the pain of grief and loss.

[2] "When a Child Dies: A Survey of Bereaved Parents." *The Compassionate Friends.* NFO Research, Inc., June 1999. Web.

[3] "Dehydration Symptoms." *Mayo Clinic.* Mayo Clinic Staff, n.d. Web.

[4] Davis, Jeanie Learche. "Can Prayer Heal?" *WebMD.* Rev. Michael W. Smith. WebMD, n.d. Web.

[5] White, Tracie. "People Who Fear Pain Are More Likely to Suffer It." *Stanford Report.* Stanford University, 1 Feb. 2006. Web.

[6] "The Bible Tops the List of the Most Read Books in the World." *RELEVANT Magazine.* 15 Nov. 2013. Web.

[7] McAllister, Dawson. "Why Do People Commit Suicide?" *TheHopeLine.* TheHopeLine, 27 Feb. 2014. Web.

ABOUT THE AUTHOR

Clara Hinton is a mom whose life has been blessed beyond measure, but has also been broken into a million pieces. She knows both the unmatched miracle of birth and the deep, unrelenting grief of child loss.

Clara has been writing for twenty years, beginning with her first book, *Silent Grief*, which continues to serve as a daily companion to those suffering the loss of a child.

In her most recent book, *Child Loss: The Heartbreak and the Hope*, Clara takes a deeper look into the complex, ongoing pain of child loss and walks those grieving the loss of a child through the foggy abyss of grief into a place of learning how to live within the ongoing pain of loss. This book is a reflection of her own heart following the sudden, unexpected loss of her son Mike, coupled with the experience of working with grieving parents for over twenty years. *The Heartbreak and the Hope* sheds new light and insights on the most misunderstood grief of all – the grief of child loss. You will never view child loss the same after reading this book! You will understand that your job is not to fix the broken heart, but rather learn how to rewrite your life story from the deep love that can only be found in brokenness.

Clara is a national speaker, certified bereavement facilitator, workshop leader, author, blogger, and grief coach. She has led workshops coast-to-coast over the past twenty years, encouraging thousands of families of child loss.

You can find Clara on Facebook at Silent Grief – Child Loss Support, where her daily posts encourage hundreds of thousands every week. She can also be found on the web at ClaraHinton.com, SilentGrief.com, and SilentGriefsupport.com. You can reach Clara by emailing her at clarahintonspeaker@gmail.com.

Look for Clara's next book coming out soon, *Grief: 365*. This book will contain one positive grief affirmation for every day of the year.

CONTRIBUTIONS

Alexandra Howlett, Clara Hinton's youngest daughter, is a yoga instructor, support group leader for survivors of sexual abuse, and marketing professional. Because of her own lifelong struggles with depression and mental illness, she has a heart for the broken and hopes to use her education and life experiences to help others along their paths to coping with emotional pain.

After the loss of her brother Mike in 2015, Alex has realized that life can change in an instant and never again be the same as it once was. Because of the uncertainty of life, she believes that learning to live through the most painful moments from a place of acceptance is an absolute must. It is then that we will have the courage and power to once again experience the new moments of beauty that life will deliver. She has contributed to *Child Loss: The Heartbreak and the Hope* to share with you some tools that will help you sit with your grief while learning to welcome the gifts of life.

You can connect with Alex at AlexHowlettYoga.com or email her at alexhowlettyoga@gmail.com.

CPSIA information can be obtained
at www.ICGtesting.com
Printed in the USA
LVOW01s1827041016
507380LV00019B/300/P